This book
belongs to

....

Grimm's Fairy Tales

Compiled by Vic Parker

Miles Kelly

First published in 2014 by Miles Kelly Publishing Ltd
Harding's Barn, Bardfield End Green, Thaxted, Essex, CM6 3PX, UK

Copyright © Miles Kelly Publishing Ltd 2014

2 4 6 8 10 9 7 5 3 1

Publishing Director Belinda Gallagher
Creative Director Jo Cowan
Editorial Director Rosie Neave
Designer Rob Hale
Production Manager Elizabeth Collins
Reprographics Stephan Davis, Jennifer Cozens, Thom Allaway

ISBN 978-1-78209-513-2

Printed in China

British Library Cataloguing-in-Publication Data
A catalogue record for this book is available from the British Library

ACKNOWLEDGEMENTS
The publishers would like to thank the following artists who have contributed to this book:
Advocate Art: Polona Kosec, Ayesha Lopez, Martina Peluso, Atyeh Zeighami
The Bright Agency: Louise Ellis, Kristina Swarner
Illustration Ltd: Laurence Cleyet-Merle (cover)
Pickled Ink: Lucia Masciullo
Plum Pudding: Mónica Carretero, Bruno Robert, Claudia Venturini

Made with paper from a sustainable forest

www.mileskelly.net
info@mileskelly.net

Contents

SPELLS AND ENCHANTMENT

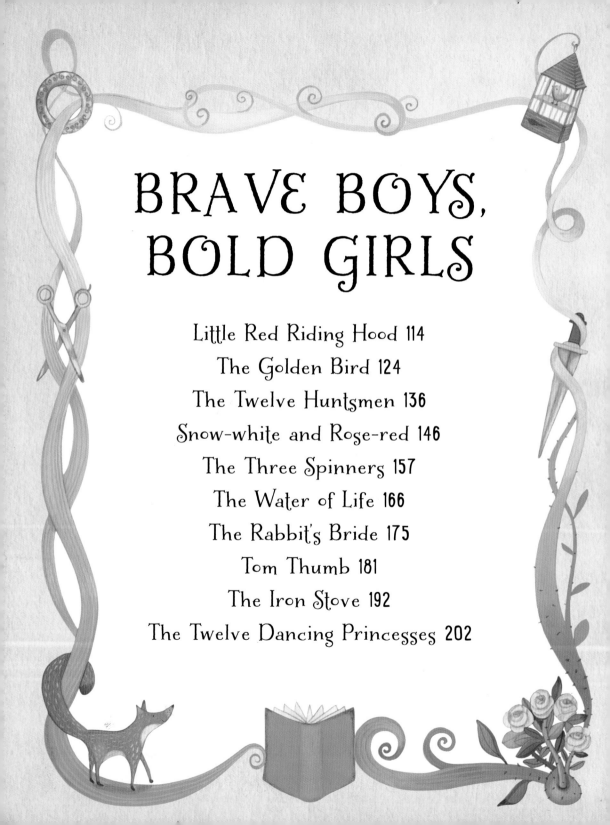

BRAVE BOYS, BOLD GIRLS

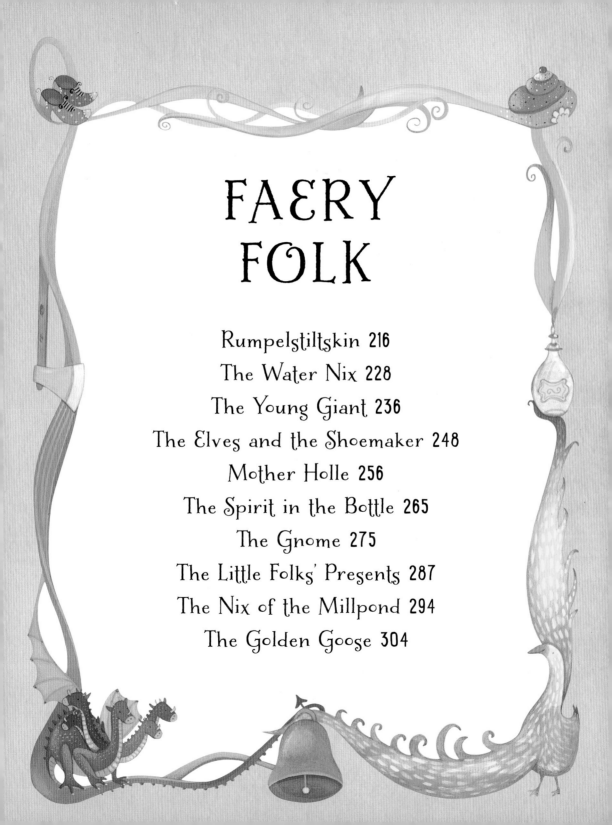

FAERY FOLK

WICKED WITCHES

HAPPY EVER AFTER

The Brothers Grimm

Once upon a time, over two hundred years ago, there lived in Germany, two brothers called Jacob and Wilhelm Grimm. They were best friends and grew up to work together, first studying law, but then becoming librarians and then university professors.

The brothers had a passion for fairy stories and folk tales – the kind that grandparents and parents had passed down to their children through generations for hundreds of years. The stories were often magical, sometimes cruel, but always gripping. The Grimm brothers wrote them down and published over 200 of them in a book.

Since then, the stories have been told in many ways in many languages. Some have become movies, plays and ballets. Here are fifty favourites retold for young children.

SPELLS AND ENCHANTMENT

The Frog Prince

Long ago, there lived a king who had three daughters. The young women were all lovely, and many princes came to seek their hands in marriage. But everyone agreed that the youngest princess was loveliest of all.

The Frog Prince

Near the royal family's castle, there was a shady wood. In summer, the youngest princess liked nothing better than to walk through the wood to a well. There she would stay, playing with a golden ball she often carried, admiring it in the dappled light.

One hot day, the princess was doing just that when her ball suddenly slipped through her fingers. It hit the ground and bounced up over the edge of the well, dropping into the water with a splash. The princess peered down inside the well, but she could see nothing but darkness. She sank down onto the mossy ground and started to cry.

"Don't upset yourself," said a croaky voice. "I can get your ball back."

The princess looked up, startled. There was no one around except for a plump frog squatting on the edge of the well. "Really?" she gasped, brightening.

"Yes, of course," reassured the frog. "But what will you give me, if I do?"

"Oh, *anything*," gushed the delighted girl. "My silver shoes… my golden purse… even my diamond tiara!"

"No, no," gulped the frog, "what would I do with those? Just promise that we will be best friends." His bulging eyes grew soft. "I want to be with you all day, every day. I want to eat with you off your golden plate, and sleep in your comfy bed. What fun we will have together!"

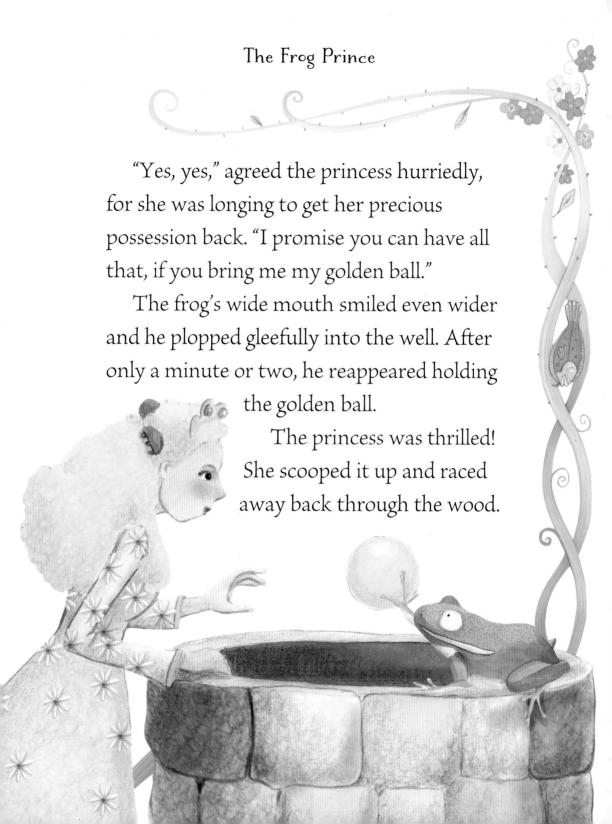

"Yes, yes," agreed the princess hurriedly, for she was longing to get her precious possession back. "I promise you can have all that, if you bring me my golden ball."

The frog's wide mouth smiled even wider and he plopped gleefully into the well. After only a minute or two, he reappeared holding the golden ball.

The princess was thrilled! She scooped it up and raced away back through the wood.

"Wait! Wait!" called the frog, leaping after her. "Pick me up! I cannot go as fast as you!"

But in her joy, the king's daughter had forgotten all about her helper. She dashed on home to the castle and the poor frog was left far behind.

That evening, when the princess and the king were eating dinner, there came a noise of something flopping wetly up the castle's staircase – *splish, splash, splish, splash!* Then there was a knocking at the door of the great hall and a voice cried, "Youngest princess, please let me in!"

Curious, the princess went to see who it could be. But when she opened the door and saw the frog sitting there, she slammed it

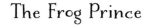

shut at once. Horrified, she sat back down without saying a word.

The king noticed that his daughter was trembling and asked, "Whatever has frightened you? Has a giant come to carry you away?" and he chuckled fondly.

But the princess grew pale. "It's no giant," she said, in a very small voice. "It's a horrid frog." And she explained what had happened the day before.

Then the knocking began again and the frog's voice said: "Youngest princess, let me in! I want what you promised me!"

The king looked grave. "You made a promise and you must keep it," he said firmly.

The youngest princess stood slowly, took a

deep breath, and went to let the frog in.

The frog hopped at her heels back to her chair. "Lift me up so I can sit with you," he croaked. The princess turned away in disgust, but the king insisted that she do as the frog had asked.

Once the frog was on the table next to the princess, he said, "Now push those golden plates a little nearer, so that we may eat together."

And the princess had to obey.

When the frog's tummy was full, he gave a yawn.

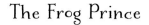

"Delicious," he said, "but now I'm tired. Let's go to bed."

Then the princess hung her head and began to weep. But the king gave her a stern look. So she picked up the slimy creature with just her finger and thumb, and held him out away from her. She carried him upstairs to her bedroom and dropped him in a corner, before quickly jumping into bed and drawing the covers over her head.

Then the frog came hopping up to her bedside, croaking, "Let me snuggle in too, or I will tell your father."

The princess groaned. She threw back the quilt and let the frog leap onto the mattress alongside her. But at the touch of his cold, damp skin she grew angry. "That's enough!" she yelled, and she seized the frog and tossed him away.

As he fell, something very strange happened. The frog began to blur and change and grow. And then, to the princess's astonishment, a handsome prince with the kindest face she had ever seen was suddenly standing in front of her. The prince smiled and gently explained how a wicked witch had enchanted him. The princess was the only one who could save him and, by carrying out her promise, she had broken the spell.

The prince knelt before the princess in thanks and, as they gazed into each other's eyes, they fell deeply in love.

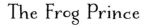

Of course, the king was delighted and gave his permission for the joyful couple to get married. And it wasn't long before they set off to the prince's kingdom in a golden carriage drawn by eight white horses, with crowds of well-wishers cheering them along the way.

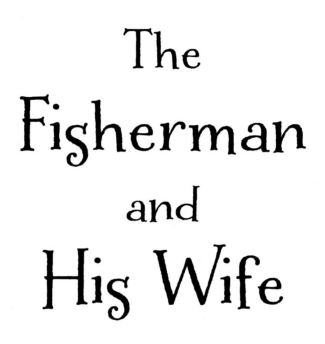

The Fisherman and His Wife

Once upon a time, there was a poor fisherman who lived with his wife in a shack by the sea. Every morning the fisherman went out fishing, and every evening he returned with only one or two little fish – just enough food to keep them from starving.

One day, the fisherman was astonished to pull up his line and see a huge flounder dangling from it.

"Hey, fisherman!" the big fish said. "I beg you, let me live. I'm not really a flounder – I'm an enchanted prince! Please let me go."

"Of course," agreed the fisherman. He put the flounder back into the water so it could swim away and he hurried home.

"Have you caught nothing at all today?" grumbled his wife.

"Not exactly," said the man. "I caught a talking flounder who said he was an enchanted prince, can you believe? He asked me to let him go so of course I did."

"Didn't you wish for anything first?" moaned the woman.

"No," said the man. "It didn't cross my mind. What could I have wished for?"

"Well, look around," sighed the woman, "it's awful to live in this shack. You might have wished for a small cottage. Go and find the flounder and ask him."

The man didn't feel comfortable about it, but his wife moaned and moaned until at last he gave in and went back to the sea. The water was no longer clear but grey and choppy as he called out:

"Flounder, flounder in the sea,
    Come, I beg you, here to me."

Then the flounder came swimming up to him and said, "Well, what do you want?"

"It's not me," said the man, "it's my wife. She does not want to live in a shack any longer. She would like a cottage."

"Go, then," said the flounder, "she has it already."

27

When the man went home, his wife was no longer in the shack, but in a little cottage. There was a porch, and pretty rooms filled with lovely furniture. Behind the cottage was a garden with hens and flowers and fruit. "Look," said the wife, "isn't this nice?"

The couple lived happily for about a fortnight, until the woman announced, "Listen, husband, I want to live in a castle. Go to the flounder and ask for one." And she moaned and moaned until at last the fisherman went back to the sea.

The sky was heavy and the waves were churning as the fisherman called out:

"Flounder, flounder in the sea,
  Come, I beg you, here to me."

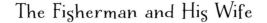

Then the flounder appeared out of the surf and said, "Well, what does your wife want now?"

"Alas," said the fisherman, feeling rather scared, "she wants to live in a castle."

"Go then, she has it," said the flounder.

Then the man went home. But instead of the cottage he found a massive stone castle. There was a great hall with servants. There were beautiful wall hangings and thick carpet. A crystal chandelier hung from the ceiling over a huge stone table laid with fine food and wine. Behind the castle there was a courtyard with stables and horses, and a magnificent park beyond.

"Look at it all!" said his wife. "Isn't this

beautiful?" And they enjoyed a feast and went to bed.

Next morning the wife prodded her husband awake and said, "Get up. I want to be king over all the land! Go to the flounder and ask him." And she moaned and moaned until at last the man went back to the sea, muttering, "It is not right…" all the way.

When he came to the sea, the sky was pitch-black. A strong wind whipped up enormous waves as the fisherman called:

"Flounder, flounder in the sea,
  Come, I beg you, here to me."

The flounder heard him and came to the shore and said, "Well, what does your wife want this time?"

"Alas," said the fisherman, "she wants to be king now."

"Go then," replied the flounder. "She is king already."

When the fisherman came to where the castle had been he saw a gleaming palace. Ranks of soldiers stood outside and, as he approached, they threw open the enormous doors. There were splendid courtiers in a magnificent hall, and his wife was sitting on a huge silver throne, wearing a golden crown on her head.

"Husband," the fisherman's wife announced. "I know I am now the king and can rule over people… but I want to be able to order the moon to rise and the sun to set –

I want to be God."

"No," said the exasperated fisherman, "I cannot ask that of the fish."

His wife grew very angry. "What!" she cried. "I am the king, and you are nothing but my husband. I order you to go and ask this instant!"

Then the fisherman was afraid, but he had to go. A great storm raged as he stood by the sea and called:

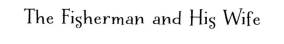

"Flounder, flounder in the sea,
   Come, I beg you, here to me."

Then the flounder rose from the crashing waves and said, "Well, what can your wife want for now?"

"Alas," whispered the fisherman, quaking, "she wants to be God."

"Go then," said the flounder, "and you will find her back again in the shack."

And there they are both still living to this very day.

The Queen Bee

Once upon a time there was a king who had three sons. When the two eldest princes grew up, they each went off into the world to seek adventures. But they both made one mistake after another, and fell

in with bad people and wasted their money, so they never made it home. The youngest prince, whom everyone called Prince Nitwit, really missed his brothers. So when he was old enough, he set off to join them.

Prince Nitwit had to work hard to find his brothers. To his surprise, when he found them at last, the two eldest princes weren't pleased to see him. "So you've tracked us down so you can have adventures too, have you?" they jeered. "Well, we're brainy and brave and we've made a mess of things, so what on earth makes you think that a simpleton like you is going to be a hero?" But eventually, after a good deal of complaining, Prince Nitwit's big brothers said they would let him travel along with them.

The three hadn't gone far when they came to an ant-hill. The two eldest princes had a nasty idea – to stir up the ant-hill with a stick, so they could laugh at the tiny insects scurrying off in terror. But Prince Nitwit wouldn't hear of it. "Leave them alone," he said. "I won't let you hurt them." His brothers grumbled about it, but at last they agreed to travel on.

They soon came to a lake where ducks were swimming. The two eldest princes discussed how they could kill some and eat them. But Prince Nitwit forbade it. "No way," he said. "We already have enough food to eat." His brothers complained about it, but

eventually they agreed to travel on.

Soon they spotted a bees' nest in a tree, overflowing with honey. The two eldest princes wanted to make a fire underneath the tree to smoke the bees out, so they could steal the honey. But Prince Nitwit would not hear of it. "Absolutely not," he said. His brothers sneered at him, but finally agreed to travel on.

One morning, the three princes came to a towering castle – but there was no sign of any people or animals anywhere. They crossed the silent drawbridge and passed the stables – all totally bare. Nervously, the princes entered the keep. Every room was furnished, just as if people were living there, but there wasn't a soul in sight!

Through empty room after empty room the princes crept, until they wandered into a huge hall where there was a stone table. The princes saw that there was some unusual writing on it. Prince Nitwit realized what it was at once. "It's instructions telling us how to release this castle from its enchantment!" he gasped, and he read aloud to his brothers what they had to do (for they weren't as good at reading as he was).

"In the wood under some moss lie one thousand pearls belonging to a princess. Find them by sunset – but if even one is missing, you will be turned into stone. Next—"

"Pah! That sounds easy enough," interrupted the eldest prince. "Leave it to me." He set off into the wood. But though he searched high and low all day, at the end of it he had found only one hundred pearls. At sunset, the last sunbeam soaked into the land, and he was turned to stone.

The second brother was determined to prove that he was braver, brainier and better than the eldest. The next day, he set off into the forest to take his turn. But alas, he did only slightly better. By sunset he had found just two hundred of the gleaming pearls and he too was turned to stone.

Poor Prince Nitwit was on his own again once more. On the morning of the third day, he set out to complete the task that his brothers had failed at, but he felt so miserable about his brothers that he hadn't found many pearls at all before he sat down and began to weep.

Suddenly, *march, march, march*! Up came the king of the ant-hill that Prince Nitwit had saved, with five thousand ant soldiers. It wasn't long at all before the little insects had collected all one thousand of the pearls and put them in a heap.

Prince Nitwit's heart lifted. He thanked the ants heartily and then hurried to read the next instruction on the table:

Fetch the key of the princesses'
sleeping-chamber out of the lake.

Prince Nitwit went and looked at the huge mirror-like expanse of water in dismay. He knew it would take him years to find the key hidden in the murky depths. But just then the two ducks whose lives he had saved came

swimming up. They upped tails and dived down to the bottom of the lake, and came up, one carrying the lost key in its beak!

Prince Nitwit was overjoyed and thanked the ducks heartily. Now all he had to do was follow the final instruction, which he now read:

Choose the youngest and loveliest of the three sleeping princesses.

But this was a truly impossible task! Prince Nitwit found the room where the three princesses lay sleeping, but they all looked equally beautiful, and each appeared to be just as young as the other! As Prince Nitwit stood there, about to despair, the Queen bee of the bees' nest that he had saved came buzzing along. The clever Queen bee remembered that before the youngest princess had been enchanted, she had eaten a spoonful of honey. She landed on the lips of each princess one by one and hovered over the one where she tasted honey.

And so it was, that Prince Nitwit made the right choice and broke the spell. The three princesses woke up and the two stone statues in the woods were changed back into Prince Nitwit's brothers. Of course, Prince Nitwit married the youngest, loveliest princess and became king, and his brothers married the other two princesses.

And that's how, thanks to the Queen bee, Prince Nitwit became the hero of a truly amazing adventure.

The Glass Coffin

There was once a young man who was learning to become a tailor, but he had always longed to have adventures, so one day he decided to go off travelling and see something of the world. But soon after he set

off he became lost in a great
forest. To make matters worse,
he suddenly heard the sound of
wild beasts roaring.

All at once a great black bull
and a beautiful stag thundered
through the trees towards
him, their horns locked in a
fight. The ground shook with their
trampling and the air rang with their
cries. For a long time the struggle
seemed even, but at last, the stag
thrust his antlers into the bull, which
fell to the ground, dead.

To the tailor's astonishment, the stag
then bounded up to him, swept him up on

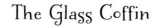

his great antlers, and carried him away. Over
mountain and valley, wood and meadow
they raced.

Just when the tailor thought he could
hold on no longer, the stag came to a stop
in front of a huge wall of rock, and gently
let him down. Then the stag drove its
antlers against a little door set into
the rock and the door sprang
open. Flames and smoke billowed
out, then a deep voice boomed:
"Enter!" The tailor drew up his courage and
plunged through.

He found himself in a huge hall with a
floor made of polished square stones. The
voice boomed again: "Stand on the broad

stone which lies in the middle of the hall."

Again the young man obeyed. He stood on the stone and it slowly gave way beneath his feet, carrying him down into the earth.

When the stone eventually stopped moving and the tailor looked around, he found himself in another hall, similar to the first. However, this hall had many hollows cut into the walls. In each one stood a glass vase, filled with blue gas. In the middle of the hall stood two big glass chests and the tailor strode over to look at them.

Inside the first was a model of a tiny castle, surrounded by a miniature village – tiny houses and farms, all perfectly detailed. Then he looked in the second glass chest. Inside lay

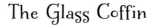

the most beautiful young woman the tailor had ever seen!

She seemed to be fast asleep. But as the tailor stood gazing at her, she suddenly opened her eyes and looked straight at him!

"Oh thank goodness!" the lovely lady cried. "Someone's here at last! Please be quick – help me out of this prison. All you have to do is push back the bolt of this glass coffin and I will be free."

The young tailor hurried to release her.

"Oh thank you!" the beautiful young woman cried, sitting up and stepping out of the glass chest. To the tailor's delight she flung her arms around him and kissed him.

"Heaven must have guided you here to

help me. Please stay with me forever! I am the daughter of a rich nobleman," she explained. "My parents died when I was young and my elder brother and I stayed living in our castle, looking after each other. We were very happy, with the kind villagers around us. Then one evening a stranger came to the castle and asked for my hand in marriage. I turned him down, which made him very angry. He muttered black magic and I fell to the ground in a faint.

"When I came to, I found myself in this cave in the glass coffin. The stranger – and by now I had realized he was a wicked magician – appeared again and said he had changed my brother into a stag. He had shrunk my castle

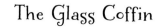

and village into a tiny model and set it in
the other glass chest. And he
had turned all
my people into
smoke and
trapped them
in glass bottles.

"He told me that he would give me
one more chance. If I would now marry him,
he would turn everything back the way it

was – all he had to do to break the spell was to get everything out of the glass… But I couldn't say yes to such an evil monster! So he vanished, leaving me here in my prison. I fell into a deep, enchanted sleep. But at last, you have arrived and set me free!

"Now please help me lift the glass chest with my castle in it on to that broad stone."

The young tailor did so at once. Immediately the stone began to rise up and up… until they were in the higher hall, and could carry the chest out into the open air. Here, the young woman opened the lid. It was amazing to watch the castle, houses, and farms quickly grow, stretch themselves and return back to their normal sizes and places.

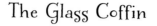

After this, the young woman and the tailor returned to the lower cave and fetched all the glass bottles.

Nervously, the lady opened them one by one. The blue smoke rushed out and instantly changed into living men, women and children. As they hugged each other, laughing delightedly, a handsome young man came striding out of the forest.

The beautiful noblewoman gasped and tears of joy sprang to her eyes. It was her brother! They ran to each other at once and the brother explained that the evil magician was gone forever. He had transformed himself into a bull whom, as the stag, the brother fought and killed. He had then

brought the young tailor here, in the hope that he would release his sister from the glass coffin. As the tailor had done so, the brother had been set free from his enchantment too.

Then everyone's joy was complete. On that very day, the beautiful noblewoman married the tailor, and they lived with her brother in the castle happily ever after.

The Magic Porridge Pot

There was once a little girl and her mother who were very poor – so poor that the day came when they no longer had anything to eat. The little girl went into the forest, crying with hunger, to see if there were any berries or nuts she could gather. As she was searching, someone came hobbling towards her through the trees. It was an old woman, carrying a little cooking pot.

"Don't cry, dear," said the old woman, kindly. "Take this little pot and go back home. Whenever you say, 'Little pot, cook!' it will cook tasty porridge." The little girl couldn't believe her eyes – porridge started to bubble up in the pot as the woman spoke. "Whenever you say, 'Little pot, stop!'" the old woman continued, "it will stop cooking." And the pot stopped cooking, full to the brim of thick, creamy porridge waiting to be eaten.

The little girl thanked the old woman wholeheartedly for her wonderful gift and hurried home with the magical pot to show her mother at once.

From then on, the little girl and her mother ate porridge whenever they wanted, and they never had empty tummies again.

One day when the little girl was out, her mother felt hungry and said, "Little pot, cook!" And the porridge instantly appeared and began to rise to the brim. But for some reason, the mother could not remember the exact words to make the pot stop. "Stop, little pot!" she ordered. But the magic pot kept cooking. "Stop, small pot!… Small pot, stop! Enough, small pot! Small pot, enough!" But still the pot kept cooking and cooking and cooking. The porridge flowed over the edge of the pot and onto the floor. And still it cooked on until the kitchen was flooded. The little pot bubbled on until the porridge spread out into the street. Then the sticky goo flowed into the house next door, and the next, and the next – and still it kept coming. Everyone was crying and wading through porridge, and no one knew how to stop it.

When the porridge was about to flood the last house in the village, the little girl came home. "Little pot, stop!" she commanded firmly – and the pot stopped cooking at once.

Then everyone had to eat the village clean!

The Donkey

Once upon a time there lived a king and a queen who were rich and had everything they wanted – except a child. Finally their wish was granted and the queen had a baby. But it was a little donkey!

The Donkey

The queen was terribly upset, but the king said bravely: "God has sent him to us. He is my son and heir to my throne. I command that no one will treat him any differently to a usual prince."

So the little donkey was brought up just the same as any royal child. The king ordered all the mirrors in the palace to be removed, so the little donkey didn't realize that he was different. He grew up happily and had a lovely nature. He liked to play and help people and he loved music, especially the lute. He studied hard and by the time he was grown up he had learned to strum the instrument with his hooves just as beautifully as any master musician.

One day, the grown-up donkey-prince was out for a walk by himself when he happened to peer into a well that was full of glassy water. He saw his own reflection for the first time – and he was shocked and horrified.

He didn't know how he could face his family and friends now that he knew what he was, and so he ran away from the palace.

He travelled far and wide, and at last

he came to a kingdom where he heard there
was an old king with a wonderfully beautiful
daughter. The donkey thought he would love
to see the princess. He trotted up to the royal
castle, sat outside the gate, took out his lute
and began playing a marvellous tune.

The king and the court were in the great
hall having dinner, and when news reached
them that a donkey sat outside the gate,
playing the lute beautifully, the king was
extremely curious. He ordered that the
donkey be brought in to dine with them at
once and for him to be seated right next to
him at the highest table.

The king made sure that the donkey was
served with the very best food and drink and

was comfortable, and the donkey kept the king entertained with his talk.

After a while, when both the donkey and the king were really enjoying themselves, the lovely princess came into the great hall. She was so beautiful that the donkey was entranced, and could not take his eyes off her. The king noticed straight away and asked, "Little donkey, do you like my daughter?"

"Oh yes," he breathed, "I have never seen anyone as beautiful as she is."

"Then you will sit next to her too," said the king.

The donkey could not believe his good luck as the king commanded his daughter to sit on the donkey's other side. The donkey-prince showed he had perfect manners, helping to serve the princess with food and drink, and charming her with polite conversation. He was kindness itself, and nothing was too much trouble.

By the end of the feast, the king liked the donkey very much and invited him to stay at the castle for as long as he wanted. By the end of a month, the king and the donkey had become firm friends. And by the end of six months, the king offered the donkey his daughter's hand in marriage. The donkey accepted with joy – for he had fallen head over heels in love with the princess.

The princess, however, was troubled. Although she had grown extremely fond of the donkey he was, after all, an animal. Who wanted a stable beast for a husband?

Still, a magnificent wedding was held with a splendid feast. The donkey was over the moon. At bedtime the donkey bolted the door of the bedchamber and checked that he and the princess were quite alone. Then, all of a sudden, he took off his donkey-skin and stood before the princess as a handsome prince. "This is who I am inside," he told her. "I have never been able to do this before, so no one has ever seen me like this."

The princess was overjoyed. She threw her arms around her handsome prince and kissed him and loved him dearly.

When morning came, the prince got up early and put his donkey-skin on again. Then he and the princess went to breakfast.

"How are you, my daughter?" whispered the old king, rather worried. "Are you sad?"

"Oh no, father," answered the princess. "I love my husband as much as if he were the most handsome man in the world, and I will do so for as long as I live."

The king was pleased, but astonished. In

fact he was so astonished that he guessed everything was not all as it seemed. That night he waited till the couple were asleep and then quietly opened the door to their bedchamber and peeked in. He was amazed to see a handsome prince lying in the bed and the donkey-skin flung on the ground. Quietly, the king took the skin away and burnt it. Then he returned to the bedchamber and stood outside the door, listening and waiting.

Early in the morning, the prince got up and went to put on his donkey-skin – but he could not find it anywhere. Then he began to panic. "Whatever will people say?" he cried in despair. "They won't believe it is me!"

But at that moment the king burst in, saying, "My son, do not worry. I know you are the donkey – and you are equally loved by me whether you are in animal form or as this handsome prince. Stay here forever. I will give you half my kingdom now and, when I die, you will rule over the whole of it."

The the prince was delighted. He even went with the princess to visit his own family, who were thrilled to see him after all that time, whether in donkey or human form. And in time, the happy couple ruled together over not just one, but two kingdoms.

The Hut in the Forest

A poor woodcutter lived with his wife and three daughters in a little hut on the edge of a forest. One morning as he was going to work, he said to his wife, "I'd better not come home for lunch today, or I will never get my work done. Ask our eldest daughter to bring it to me in the forest. To show which way I've gone, I will sprinkle millet seeds on the path."

So, when the sun was high, the girl set out. However, the birds had already pecked up the millet seeds and she could not find the track. Bravely, she went on, until night fell. The trees rustled in the darkness, the owls hooted, and she was afraid. Then in the distance she saw a light glimmering and she headed towards it.

She came to a little house and knocked. A rough voice cried, "Come in."

When the girl opened the door, an old grey-haired man with a long white beard was

sitting at a table. Next to a stove were three animals: a hen, a cockerel, and a brindled cow. The girl begged for shelter for the night and the man said:

"Little hen, little cockerel, and little brindled cow, what do you say to that?"

"Very well," answered the animals.

And the old man said, "You can stay with us and share our supper. But first, you have to cook it."

The girl was relieved and gladly prepared a tasty meal – however, she didn't think of the animals. She carried two dishes to the table, sat by the grey-haired man, and ate.

Then, she said, "Is there a bed for me?"

But the animals replied, "You didn't think about us, so find out for yourself."

The old man said, "Go upstairs and you'll find a room with a bed."

So the girl went up to bed, without further thought. After some time, however, the grey-haired man came up and looked at the girl and shook his head, sadly. Then he opened a trap-door and the girl found herself slipping and sliding down a dark tunnel until she came to land in the cold cellar.

Late that night the woodcutter came home and told his wife off for leaving him hungry all day.

"It is not my fault," she replied, "our daughter must have got lost! We can only hope she finds her way back tomorrow."

Next day the woodcutter asked that their second daughter should take him his lunch. "I will leave lentils on the track," said he; "the seeds are larger than millet. The girl will see them better and won't lose her way."

So at lunchtime the girl went out with the food, but once again the birds had already pecked up the lentils. She wandered about until night and then she too reached the house of the grey-haired old man. She was invited in and begged for food and a bed. Everything happened just as it had the day before. The girl cooked a good meal, ate and drank with the old man, and did not think about the animals. And when she was asleep the old man came, looked at her, shook his head, and let her down into the cellar.

On the third morning the woodcutter said to his wife, "Send our youngest child with my lunch today. I will leave peas on the track. They are even larger than lentils – she can't miss those."

But when the girl went out, the birds had already pecked up the peas. She wandered about until it grew dark, and she saw the light and came to the hut. She begged to spend the night there, and the grey-haired old man once more asked his animals. "Very well," they said.

Then the girl stroked the smooth feathers of the cockerel and the hen, and patted the brindled cow between her horns. Next she prepared some soup for the grey-haired man and herself. When it was ready, she first served barley for the cockerel and hen, a whole armful of sweet-smelling hay for the brindled cow, and fetched a bucketful of water for the animals to drink. Only then did she sit down and begin to eat her own food.

Afterwards, the animals said: "You have looked after us kindly and we wish you a very good night."

So the girl went upstairs, found the bed, and fell sound asleep.

At midnight, there was such a noise that she woke up suddenly. There was the sound of cracking and splitting in every corner. The beams groaned, the staircase creaked and there was a crash as if the roof had fallen in. Then all suddenly grew quiet.

As the girl was not hurt, she stayed quietly lying where she was and fell asleep again. But when she woke up in the morning, what did she see? She was lying in a splendid palace bedroom! The girl thought she must be dreaming. She got up to make breakfast for the old man, and to feed the hen, the cockerel and the brindled cow.

She went down
the staircase and found,
not the old man but a handsome young
stranger. He told her, "I am a prince.
A witch turned me into an old man and my
three servants into a cockerel, a hen and a

cow. The spell could only be broken by a girl like you, whose heart is full of love for all living things. At midnight we were set free and the hut changed back into my palace. Your sisters have been set free too. They will live with your parents until they learn to look after all creatures. Now, I beg you to live here with me forever as my wife. "

As the girl looked at the prince's kind face, she fell in love and agreed. And so they were married and lived together happily in the prince's palace, and the kind girl visited her family whenever she wanted.

The Singing, Soaring Lark

Once there was a man who was about to set out on a long journey. While saying goodbye to his three daughters, he asked what gifts they would like him to bring them. The eldest wished for pearls. The second wished for diamonds. But the third said, "Dear father, I should like a singing, soaring lark." He kissed all three and set out.

However, when the time came for him to return, he was very sad. He had brought pearls and diamonds, but he had not been able to find a singing, soaring lark.

The man was riding through a forest on his way home when he suddenly noticed a singing, soaring lark on a tree-top. Delighted, he went to try and catch it. But a lion leapt out and roared: "I will EAT whoever tries to steal my singing, soaring lark!"

"Forgive me," begged the trembling man.

The lion said, "I will let you live if you swear to give me the first thing that comes to

meet you when you get back to your home. If you promise me that, I will give you my lark into the bargain."

The man was very frightened, but he had no choice. He promised the lion what he wanted.

When the man reached home, he was horrified to see his youngest daughter running up to him. She threw her arms around him – and when she saw that he had a singing, soaring lark, she was beside herself with joy. The father, however, began to weep, and explained his terrible promise.

Fortunately, his daughter was very brave as well as beautiful, and the next morning, she headed down the road to the lion's castle.

Little did the girl know that the lion was not really a lion at all – he was an enchanted prince! He was only a lion by day. At night, he changed back to his human form.

When the girl arrived, the lion welcomed her gently and warmly, making her most fond of him. And at night, when the lion turned into a handsome prince, she fell in love with him. They were soon married and lived happily together, staying awake at night, and sleeping during the daytime. The only thing the girl still found strange was that there were no candles in the castle, there were only flaming torches for light.

One night the prince told his wife: "Tomorrow, your eldest sister is getting married. Would you like to go?"

"Oh yes," she replied, her eyes shining, "I would love to – and you must come, too."

The lion sadly explained that it was too dangerous for him – as part of the enchantment, if candlelight fell on him, he would be changed into a dove for seven years.

"Oh come with me," she begged, "I will protect you from all candlelight."

When the girl arrived at her father's house there was great joy, for everyone

believed that she had been torn to pieces by
the lion! But she explained to them how
handsome her husband truly was and how
well off they were, and the lion was
welcomed just as she was. The wedding took
place and, when night was falling and candles
were about to be lit for the feast, the girl
showed her husband to a stone chamber so
strong and thick that no light could pierce it.

However, she did not notice that the door
was made of wood, and it had a tiny chink in
it. As soon as the first candle was lit, a tiny
ray of candlelight passed through and fell on
the prince.

When the feast was over and every candle
was put out, the girl went to see her husband

by torchlight. To her horror, she found only a white dove, which said to her: "Alas, now I must fly over the world for seven years!" and flew out of the door.

The girl hurried to follow. For years she travelled, never taking her eyes off the dove or resting. But on the very last day of the seven years, the dove flew so high and fast that it disappeared!

"Have you seen the dove?" The girl called desperately to the sun.

And the sun replied: "The white dove has flown to the Red Sea, where it has become a lion again, for the seven years are over. But it is fighting there with a dragon, who is really an enchanted princess. Go and find the lion,

then count the reeds by the sea. Cut off the eleventh and strike the dragon with it. The lion will win the fight and both he and the dragon will turn back to their human forms. Then you and your husband can spring onto a griffin who will be standing nearby – he will fly you over the sea back home." And the sun gave the girl a casket to take with her. "Open this if you think you need to," he said.

So the brave girl journeyed to the Red Sea. She counted the reeds, cut off the eleventh and struck the dragon with it. It immediately became weaker, so that the lion overcame it – and both beasts turned back into the prince and princess they really were. But before the girl could run to her husband and hug him, the wicked princess sprang onto the griffin's back, seized the prince's arm and flew off with him!

Broken-hearted, the girl travelled for many more months down long, hard roads until at last she came to the castle where the wicked princess lived. Then she opened the casket that the sun had given her and discovered within it a dress that sparkled and glittered like sunbeams. She put it on and knocked at the gate.

When everyone saw her, they stared in astonishment – even the wicked princess.

"I am soon to be married," she told the girl, "and I *must* have that dress to wear for my wedding. What will you sell it for?"

Then the girl answered boldly: "Not for money. I will only sell it for a night in the room where your husband-to-be sleeps."

The wicked princess longed so much for the amazing dress that she agreed.

That night, the girl was shown to a bedroom where her husband lay in a deep, magical sleep. "I followed you for seven years," she whispered to him. "I asked the sun where you were. I helped you defeat a dragon. Please wake up and tell me you haven't forgotten me..."

The sound of his wife's voice broke into his enchanted dreams – and the prince woke up! "Now I am really released!" he cried with joy, hugging and kissing her. They both crept

out of the castle while everyone was asleep,
found the griffin, and flew off back home,
where they finally lived happily ever after.

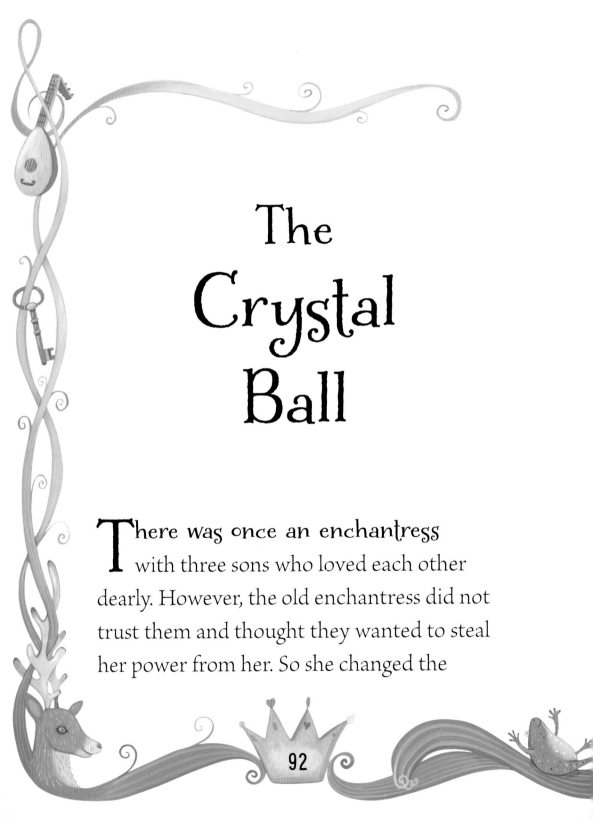

The Crystal Ball

There was once an enchantress with three sons who loved each other dearly. However, the old enchantress did not trust them and thought they wanted to steal her power from her. So she changed the eldest into an eagle, and he had to fly away and live in the mountains. She changed the second into a whale, and he was forced to live in the sea. But the third son managed to run away before his wicked mother turned him into a beast too.

At first the third son didn't know what to do with himself without his beloved brothers. But then he decided to rescue a king's daughter who was bewitched and imprisoned in a castle called the Castle of the Golden Sun. Many young men had already died trying. Still, the youngest son was brave and made up his mind to do his best.

He travelled for a long time seeking the castle, but he could not find it. One day, he was going through a forest when he came across two arguing giants, one of them holding a hat. "We both want the hat," one giant explained. "We cannot decide who it rightfully belongs to!"

"How can you fall out so badly about a hat?" asked the youth.

"It is no ordinary hat," said the second giant. "It is a wishing-hat. Whoever wears it can wish himself wherever he wants to go and in an instant he will be there."

Then the young man said, "Give me the hat. I will walk a short distance off and shout 'Go!'. You two start running and whoever reaches me first will win the hat."

The giants thought this was a brilliant idea and they gave him the wishing-hat. So the young man walked away and put on the hat and thought of the Castle of the Golden Sun. Immediately he found himself standing on a high mountain in front of the castle gate. He entered and climbed to the top of the highest tower, where he found the king's daughter. But how shocked he was. She had a wrinkly, grey face, red eyes and lank, greasy hair.

"Are you the king's daughter whom everyone says is so beautiful?" he asked politely, trying to hide his surprise.

"Yes," she answered, "but this is not what I really look like. I have been bewitched so I appear ugly." She held up a mirror. In it the young man saw himself reflected next to the most beautiful young lady in the world. "This is what I really look like," she explained, with tears rolling down her cheeks.

"However can I break the spell and set you free?" he urged.

And the princess said, "Go down the mountain and you will see a wild bull standing by a stream. You must fight it. Many young men have died trying. If you can kill it, a fiery bird will spring out of it. Inside the bird's body is a strange egg. And

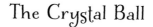

inside the egg is a crystal ball which holds the magic of the enchanter who bewitched me.

"If you can catch the fiery bird and get the crystal ball, bring it here to the enchanter in the great hall. His power will be destroyed. But the bird will burn you if you touch it. And if the egg falls on the ground it will blaze into flame and burn everything nearby with it, including the crystal ball."

So the youth went down the mountain to the stream. There stood the bull, snorting and bellowing. The bull charged at the young man, but he grabbed its horns and swung onto its back. As it tried to throw him off, he drew his sword, plunged it into the animal, and it fell down dead.

Straight away
a fiery bird flew
out of it, but it soared
away into the sky. Just as
the young man thought all
hope was lost an eagle – the young man's
brother – suddenly swooped down from the
clouds and hunted the fiery bird out to sea.

When at last the bird was exhausted at
being chased, it let its egg fall. The egg landed

on a fisherman's hut on the shore, which immediately burst into flames.

The young man started to despair once more, but then a whale came swimming towards the shore – it was the young man's other brother. It made a huge wave which surged over the hut and put out the flames.

When all was safe the youth hurried to look for the egg in the ruins. Luckily, it had not been totally destroyed – only the shell had melted, and he was able to take out the crystal ball unharmed.

Carefully, he carried it back to the Castle of the Golden Sun. He strode into the great hall, where the enchanter sat poring over his book of black magic, and held the crystal ball before him.

Then the sorcerer gave a cry of despair and disappeared in a flash of green fire.

The young man's heart soared. He hurried to find the king's daughter and, when he entered her room, he found her sitting there as her true, beautiful self. Next, he used the

magic of the crystal ball to turn his faithful brothers back to their human form. Then they all lived happily in the Castle of the Golden Sun with the magic crystal ball to protect them, so no enchantresses or enchanters ever bothered them again.

Sleeping Beauty

Long ago, a king and queen reigned in a country far away. They waited a long time to have a child, and when the queen finally gave birth to a little girl, everyone in the land rejoiced. The proud king held a feast to celebrate. He invited all his family and nobles and friends and neighbours. And the joyful queen said, "We should invite the fairies too, so that they will always be kind and good to our little daughter."

Now there were thirteen fairies in the kingdom, but the king and queen had only twelve golden dishes for them to eat out of. So the royal couple decided not to invite one of the fairies.

The big day came and the twelve fairies arrived, each with a long white wand in her hand. And after the feast was over they gathered round the baby's cradle and each gave her a gift: goodness, beauty, intelligence, and so on – all the best things in the world.

Just as eleven of the fairies
had finished, a great noise
was heard in the courtyard.
Into the feasting hall strode
the thirteenth fairy, with a
broomstick in her hand. As
she had not been invited to
the feast she was very angry.
She swept up to the cradle and
cried out: "When the
princess is fifteen

she shall be injured by a spinning wheel spindle and fall down dead."

The queen collapsed into the king's arms in shock, while everyone gasped and wept and wrung their hands, and the evil fairy stormed out.

Everyone had quite forgotten the twelfth of the friendly fairies, who had not yet given her gift. Now she stepped forward. "I'm afraid I cannot undo the evil curse," she sighed, "but perhaps I can soften it a little…" And she made a magic wish: that the princess would not die when the spindle injured her, only fall asleep for a hundred years.

The next day, the king did what he could to save his dear child: he ordered that all the spinning wheels in the kingdom should be burnt. And so the little princess grew up without ever seeing one. She became good and clever and beautiful– and all the other wonderful things the eleven good fairies had wished for her. Everyone who knew her, loved her.

On the day of her fifteenth birthday, the princess was walking through the palace when she came across a little door she had never noticed before. She opened it and there was the entrance to a mysterious tower. At the top of the tower steps sat an old lady, busy at a strange wheel with some thread.

"Hello," said the princess, very curious. "What are you doing?"

"Spinning,"
said the old lady,
and hummed a
tune while *whrrr!*
went the wheel.

"How prettily
that little thing
turns round!"
said the princess,
reaching out for
the spindle. "Ouch!"
she cried as her fingers
touched it.

And while the wicked fairy (for it was
she) and her spinning wheel vanished, the
princess fell down in an enchanted sleep.

At that moment the king and queen on their thrones in the great hall fell asleep too, and so did all the courtiers. The dogs slept by their feet, and so did the horses in the stables, the pigeons on the tops of the turrets and the flies upon the walls. In the kitchen the butler fell asleep while taking a drink of beer and the cook fell asleep while turning a goose on a spit – even the fire on the hearth stopped blazing. In the courtyard and gardens the fountains froze, the flowers stilled, and the royal guards nodded and slept soundly.

Days, weeks and then months went past and a large hedge of thorns soon grew round the palace. Every year it became higher and thicker, till at last the palace was surrounded and hidden, so that not even the roof or the chimneys could be seen. But people often told stories of the beautiful sleeping Briar Rose (for so the king's daughter was called). And from time to time, princes would find the thicket and try to break through to reach the palace. No one ever could, however, for the thorns and bushes grabbed them as if they had hands and held them fast.

On the very day that one hundred years had passed, a prince was riding near the thicket. To his astonishment the bushes parted as he approached to let him clamber through easily, and the sharp thorns turned into beautiful flowers as he passed them.

He came to the palace and walked

through the still courtyard, the silent gardens and the motionless halls, marvelling at how everything and everyone had been frozen in time. Finally, he passed through a strange little door and came to the small tower room where Princess Briar Rose lay asleep on the floor. She looked so beautiful that the prince stooped down and gave her a kiss.

At that moment she opened her eyes and woke up. And how she smiled at the handsome prince before her! He helped her up and together they went out into the palace – in which everyone else was waking up too, quite astonished.

Over the coming days, an even more splendid feast was held than at Briar Rose's

birth – a feast to celebrate her marriage to the prince. And everyone lived happily ever after.

BRAVE BOYS, BOLD GIRLS

Little Red Riding Hood

Once upon a time there was a little girl who was so kind and good that everyone loved her. Her grandmother gave her a special present – a hooded travelling cloak of red velvet. The little girl

thought it was so beautiful that from then on she never went out in anything else. So everyone called her 'Little Red Riding Hood.'

One day, the girl's mother said: "Little Red Riding Hood, your grandmother is ill. Will you visit her and take her this bottle of juice and her favourite cake? Hopefully they will do her good. Now, you know the way very well – make sure you don't leave the path, go straight there."

"Don't worry, mother," said Little Red Riding Hood, "I'll go straight there." She took the juice and cake and off she set through the woods to her grandmother's house.

She hadn't gone very far when a wolf trotted out of the trees up to her. Little Red

Riding Hood did not know that the wolf was sly and dangerous, so she wasn't at all afraid.

"Hello, Little Red Riding Hood," said the wolf, politely.

"Good day, Mr Wolf," said Little Red Riding Hood, and the wolf began to walk beside her.

"Where are you going?" he grinned.

"To my grandmother's," Little Red Riding Hood replied. "She's ill so I'm taking her some treats to help her feel better."

"And where does your grandmother live, Little Red Riding Hood?" asked the wolf.

"Just a few minutes further on," the girl replied. "Her cottage is the little one underneath the three large oak trees, you must have seen it."

Little Red Riding Hood never dreamed that the wolf was up to no good, but he was actually thinking:

117

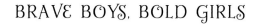

'This little girl is so young and sweet, she would taste delicious! Maybe I can eat the grandma first, to stop my empty stomach rumbling, then this little girl second, as a sweet pudding…'

He quickly thought up a plan to slow Little Red Riding Hood down and be the first to reach the cottage. "How pretty the flowers are here," he remarked. "Why don't you pick some for your grandmother?"

"What a lovely idea," said Little Red Riding Hood, "thank you, Mr Wolf." And she skipped off into the trees to gather a pretty posy, while the wolf bounded off down the path, as fast as his legs could carry him.

Very soon he reached the grandmother's cottage and knocked gently at the door.

"Who's there?" came the sick old lady's weak, trembly voice.

The wolf tried to make his voice sound like Little Red Riding Hood's. "It's your granddaughter," he squeaked. "I've brought some treats for you. Open the door."

"How lovely – thank you!" called out the grandmother. "But I'm afraid I'm too weak to get up – just let yourself in."

The wolf licked his lips. He lifted the latch and pushed the door open. He sprang over to the grandmother's bed and swallowed her up with one *snap* of his jaws. Then he squeezed into her frilly nightdress and cap, drew the curtains together to darken the room, and lay down in her bed, pulling the covers over his chin.

Little Red Riding Hood arrived at the cottage to find the door wide open. 'How strange!' she thought. Nervously, she stepped inside to find the usually bright room all dim and gloomy. 'Very strange indeed,' she thought. There lay her grandmother with her nightcap pulled far down over her face and the covers drawn up over her chin, looking very odd.

"Oh, Grandmother," Little Red Riding

Hood said, "what big ears you have! I've never noticed before."

"All the better to hear you with, my dear," came the reply.

"Oh, Grandmother, what big eyes you have!" Little Red Riding Hood couldn't help but remark.

"All the better to see you with, my dear," came the reply.

"Oh, Grandmother, what large hands you have!" said Little Red Riding Hood, her eyes widening with surprise.

"All the better to hug you with, my dear," came the reply.

"Oh Grandmother! What a big mouth you have!" gasped Little Red Riding Hood.

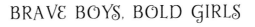

"All the better to eat you with!" roared the wolf. And with that, he sprang out of bed and swallowed Little Red Riding Hood up.

The wolf now had such a full stomach that he began to feel very sleepy. Quite pleased with himself, he lay back down in the bed for a snooze.

But while he was snoring, a huntsman passed the cottage. The man thought it very unusual that the door was open wide and he looked in to see if everything was all right.

His eyes lit up when he saw the wolf in the bed. 'Ah, I have been trying to catch you for a long time!' he thought. He took out his hunting knife and – *slash, slash* – that was the end of the wicked creature… and out of the slit in the wolf's tummy came Little Red Riding Hood and her grandmother! The wolf had swallowed them whole so, apart from being frightened, they were quite unharmed.

Then all three were delighted. The huntsman went home carrying the wolfskin. The grandmother admired the flowers, drank the juice and ate the cake and began to feel much better. And Little Red Riding Hood ran home safely to her mother and lived happily ever after.

The Golden Bird

There was once a king who had a beautiful garden with a tree which grew golden apples. Every day, it was the royal gardener's job to count the apples. But one morning, one was missing. It was the same the next morning… and the next. The king was angry, so the gardener told his son to keep watch all night under the tree and see what was happening.

At midnight the young man heard a rustling noise. A golden bird came flying through the darkness. The gardener's son jumped up with his bow and arrow. As the golden bird snapped one of the apples into its beak, he let fly a shot. But the arrow only zipped through the bird's tail and a single feather fell to the ground.

Next morning, the gardener told the king what his son had seen and presented him with the golden feather. The king was stunned and called his wisest advisors to take a look. Everyone agreed it was worth more than the king's whole treasure house. "I must have the whole bird!" ordered the king, greedily. So the gardener's son set out to find it.

He travelled in the direction the bird had flown until he came to the edge of a wood where a fox was sitting. "Sit upon my tail and you will travel faster," said the fox. The young man did so and away they sped over hills and fields.

Near a huge castle, the fox stopped.

"The soldiers are asleep," he told the gardener's son. "In a room you'll find the golden bird in a wooden cage. There will be an empty golden cage nearby, but don't try and swap the bird into that one or you'll wish you hadn't."

So the young man approached the castle, crept past the sleeping soldiers, and found the room with the golden bird. It was so beautiful that he couldn't bear to bring it away in such a dull old cage, and he swapped it into the golden cage after all. As he did so the bird let out an ear-splitting scream! The soldiers woke and took him prisoner and hauled him before the king.

"You will die for stealing my golden bird," announced the king, "unless you can bring me the golden horse. If you can do that, I will set you free – and I will let you take the golden bird too."

The gardener's son went back to the fox, ashamed. "Why didn't you do as I said?" scolded the fox. But he allowed the young man to climb onto his tail once more, and raced off with him to another castle. "Go into the stables and you'll find the golden horse," said the fox. "His groom will be asleep. But put the old leather saddle on the horse, not the golden one that is nearby."

So the young man crept into the stables, past the sleeping groom, and found the golden horse. He was so beautiful that he couldn't bear to put the old leather saddle on him, so instead he put the golden one on after all. As he did so the groom woke and shouted for the guards, who took the young man prisoner and hauled him before the king.

"You will die for stealing my golden horse," announced the king, "unless you can bring me the beautiful princess. If you can do that, I will set you free – and I will let you take the golden horse too."

So the gardener's son went back to the fox, even more ashamed. "Why didn't you do as I said?" scolded the fox, and raced off with him to a third castle. "At midnight, the princess will come out to bathe in the lake," the fox

explained. "Go and give her a kiss and she'll come with you willingly – but make sure you don't let her go and say goodbye to her mother and father."

So the young man waited till midnight – and just as the fox had said, out came the princess to bathe in the lake. He went and gave her a kiss and she agreed to go away with him. However, she begged to go and say goodbye to her parents – and she was so beautiful that the gardener's son couldn't bear to refuse.

Of course the very moment the couple entered the castle, guards seized him for trying to steal the princess and hauled him before the king.

"You will die for stealing my daughter," announced the king, "unless in eight days you can dig away the hill that blocks the view from my window. If you can do that, I will set you free – and I will let you take my daughter too."

So the gardener's son hung his head in shame and started digging. After seven days the hill was hardly any smaller. Then the fox came to him and said, "Why didn't you do as I said? But lie down and go to sleep, I will work for you."

In the morning the young man awoke to find that the hill was entirely gone! The king could not believe his eyes, but he had to keep his promise and he allowed the gardener's son

to leave with the beautiful princess.

"Now listen very carefully," the fox said to the gardener's son, "and I will tell you how you can keep all three: the princess, the horse and the bird."

This time, the gardener's son was determined not to make any mistakes. He did exactly as the fox said.

First, he took the beautiful princess to the king who wanted her. To his delight, the golden horse was brought out to him and he immediately leapt onto its back.

He reached down to the princess as though he wished to kiss her hand to say goodbye, but in one quick movement he seized her wrist, swung her up onto the

The Golden Bird

horse's back behind him,
spurred his steed on, and they were off,
as swift as the wind.

Then he took the golden horse to the
king who wanted him. To his delight, the
golden bird was brought out. "I must check
that it really is the right bird," the gardener's

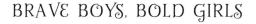

son said – and as soon as the bird was in his hands he spurred the horse on once more, and they were off, as swift as the wind.

Finally, they took the golden bird to the king who wanted him. The king was so delighted that he not only let the gardener's son keep the golden horse and marry the beautiful princess, he also made him heir to his kingdom!

Then the fox came to him and said: "Now you must kill me. Trust me and do as I say." The young man did not want to do this at all, but he trusted the fox. He took a sword and did exactly as he had been told. At once there was a blinding flash and suddenly a handsome prince stood before him – it was the princess's long-lost brother, finally free from an evil enchantment that had been put upon him many years ago. Then everyone's joy was complete and they all lived happily ever after.

The Twelve Huntsmen

There was once a prince who lived
in a palace near his father's castle. The
prince fell in love with a certain princess and
wished to marry her. He even gave her a ring
as a sign that they were to be wed. But before

he could give his father the good news that he was engaged, a messenger arrived from the castle with news that the king had fallen seriously ill.

The prince hurried to his father's castle and found that his father was dying.

"My son," the king gasped, "here is… my last wish. I want you… to marry…" and he named a princess who lived in a far-off land.

The prince was so upset to see his father dying that he could not think straight about what he was doing. "Of course," he said, seeking to comfort the old man, "I will do as you wish."

And the king shut his eyes and died.

Over the next few weeks everyone wore

black and wept for the old king. Then the prince was crowned the new ruler. Next, the news was announced that the new king was going to marry the princess from the far-off land and that she was already on her way to the castle.

When the princess who was already engaged to the prince heard this, she cried as if she would never stop. Her father hated to see her so upset. "However can I help you feel better?" he begged. "Whatever you want, I'll get it for you."

But the princess didn't want cheering up – she just wanted her dear prince once more. So she thought hard and said: "Father, I would like you to find me eleven girls – but they must look exactly like me."

Her father was puzzled but he ordered his servants to search far and wide. Soon eleven young women were found who looked exactly like his daughter. Then the princess asked for twelve suits of huntsmen's clothes to be made and she and the other eleven girls put them on. She said goodbye to her father and she and the girls set off on horseback to her sweetheart's castle.

The disguised princess boldly asked to see the king. Her heart fluttered as she saw her beloved, but he did not recognize her. The princess asked if he needed any huntsmen. The king thought the twelve men looked so smart that he found himself saying yes.

Now the king had a pet lion who knew all sorts of secrets. That evening, as the lion sat at the king's feet, he looked up at his master and said: "Your twelve new huntsmen are actually twelve girls."

"No, surely not!" said the king in great surprise. "Prove it."

"All right," said the lion. "Order some peas to be scattered in the hallway. Men have a firm step, so when they step on the peas they will squash them. But girls will trip and slip."

The king thought that was a great idea and ordered the peas to

140

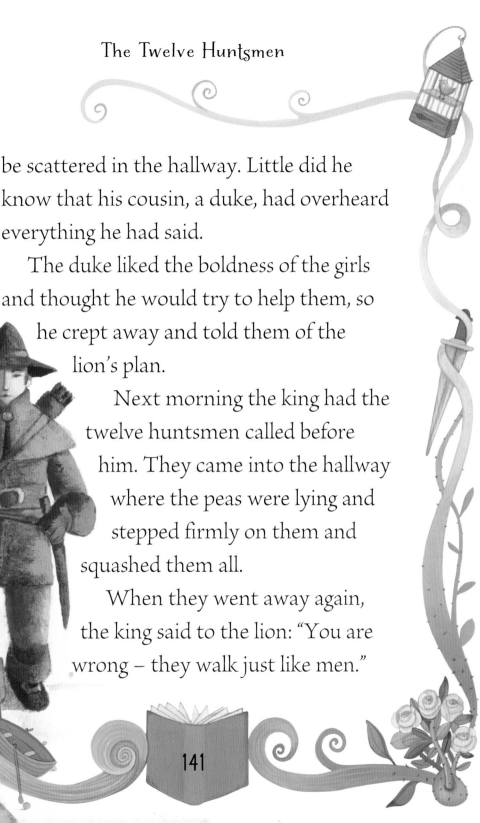

be scattered in the hallway. Little did he know that his cousin, a duke, had overheard everything he had said.

The duke liked the boldness of the girls and thought he would try to help them, so he crept away and told them of the lion's plan.

Next morning the king had the twelve huntsmen called before him. They came into the hallway where the peas were lying and stepped firmly on them and squashed them all.

When they went away again, the king said to the lion: "You are wrong – they walk just like men."

141

The lion replied calmly, "Someone must have told them about our plan with the peas." But the king had lost patience and no longer believed him.

The next day, the king called for the twelve huntsmen to lead him on a hunt through the forest, and they all set off. As they were riding through the trees, a messenger rode out to meet them with news that the king's new bride would be arriving at the castle that very day.

When the princess heard this, she felt as though her heart were breaking and she fell to the ground in a faint. The king raced at once to the fallen figure, thinking that the brave captain of his huntsmen had been taken gravely ill. He sprang off his horse and bent over her, taking off the huntsman's helmet and gloves.

When he saw the lovely face of his princess and recognized his ring on her finger, he gasped in surprise and joy. "Forgive me, father," he murmured, "but I cannot marry the other princess. I am sure if I had been able to tell you about my true love, you would have been very happy for me to marry her."

Then he kissed his true sweetheart and, when she opened her eyes, he told her: "You are mine, and I am yours, and nothing will ever keep us apart."

Immediately, the king sent a messenger to explain to the princess from the far-off land

that he was very sorry that she had travelled all that way but he could no longer marry her.

As luck would have it she wasn't disappointed at all. She had arrived at the castle and immediately met the duke, with whom she had fallen in love straight away.

And so two weddings were celebrated instead of one – and they

144

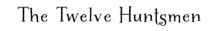

were very grand and happy affairs indeed. Hundreds of guests ate, drank and danced for three days and nights, and the lion was the guest of honour, of course.

Snow-white
and
Rose-red

There was once a poor widow who lived in a little cottage. In front of the cottage was a garden in which stood two rose-trees, one with white roses and one with red roses. The widow had two children who were like the two rose-trees. She named them Snow-white and Rose-red. They grew up to be good and kind, and all the creatures of the meadows and forests were their friends. The girls did everything together and promised never to leave each other. Every day, they kept their home neat and tidy. In the evening, the little family sat around the fire, reading stories to each other.

One winter's evening there was a knock at the door. The mother said, "Rose-red, go and see who it is, it must be a traveller in need of shelter for the night." But it wasn't – it was a big, black bear!

The girls screamed, but the bear said gently, "Don't be afraid, I won't hurt you!

I am half frozen – all I want is to warm up a little in front of your fire."

"Poor bear," said the mother, "come and lie down by the hearth."

So the bear stretched himself out, to melt the snow from his coat.

By and by, Snow-white and Rose-red grew less afraid. They fetched the broom and brushed his shaggy fur, and soon they were quite comfortable with him. They scratched his back and stroked his head, and he rolled over and let them tickle his tummy.

When it was bedtime, the mother let the bear sleep by the hearth. And when day dawned, the two girls let him out and he padded back into the forest.

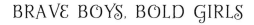

All winter, the bear came every evening at the same time. Then one day, spring arrived. That morning, the bear said: "Now I must go away and I cannot visit you again for the whole summer."

"But where will you go, dear bear?" asked Snow-white.

"Into the forest, to guard it from wicked dwarfs. In the winter, they have to stay under the frozen ground. But now, the sun is warming the earth and they will soon break through it."

The girls were very sad, but the bear promised to return at wintertime.

A week later, the sisters went into the forest to fetch firewood. Near a fallen tree, they saw a little man jumping about in the grass. It was an angry dwarf, who had got the end of his long beard caught in a split in the tree trunk. Snow-white was carrying scissors in the pocket of her apron and she hurried over to help. She cut off the end of the beard, freeing him.

"You stupid girl! You've cut off a piece of my beard!" the dwarf cried, most ungratefully. "Bad luck to you!" And he grabbed a bag of gold which lay among the roots of the tree and dashed off without a backward glance.

'How rude', thought Snow-white and Rose-red.

A few days afterwards, the sisters went to

catch fish for their supper. As they came near to the brook they saw a little man jumping about at the water's edge. It was the dwarf again! He had been fishing, but his line had caught in his beard and a fish was doing its best to pull him into the water.

Once again, the girls hurried to help him. Quickly and carefully, Rose-red took out her fishing knife and sliced through the beard.

"How dare you cut off even more of my beard!" the dwarf roared, his face like thunder. "Double bad luck to you!" He snatched up a sack of pearls that lay in the rushes and disappeared behind a stone.

Soon afterwards, the mother sent the girls to town to buy needles and thread. The road led across a flat, rocky heath. They noticed a large bird hovering in the air, then suddenly it swooped down and they heard a loud cry. The sisters ran over and saw with horror that an eagle had seized their old friend the dwarf and was going to carry him off.

The girls grabbed hold of the little man and pulled against the eagle so hard that at last it let go and flew off. "Couldn't you have been more careful? You've ripped my coat to pieces!" he yelled, hopping mad. "Triple bad luck to you!" And he heaved up a sack full of precious jewels and slipped away under a rock into the earth.

The girls never imagined that on their way home they would stumble across the dwarf again. But there he was, sitting on the rocky heath. He had emptied out his bag of precious stones and was admiring them in the setting sun. They sparkled so beautifully that the girls stood still and stared at them.

"Why do you stand gaping there?" cried the dwarf, his face turning red with rage. He was about to curse the sisters for the fourth time when, with a loud growl, a black bear came galloping out of the forest. The dwarf sprang up in a fright and begged: "Dear Mr Bear, please spare me! I will give you all my treasure, I promise. Eat these two girls instead, please. They're much bigger and tastier than me."

But the bear took no notice. He killed the evil dwarf with one swipe of his paw – and that was the end of him.

The girls stood trembling, hand in hand. They shut their eyes and waited for the bear to strike them too. But to their astonishment he spoke to them. He said: "Snow-white and Rose-red, do not be afraid."

At once they recognized his voice and opened their eyes. As the bear walked towards them his bearskin fell off and there stood a handsome man, dressed in gold. "I am a king's son," he said, "and I was bewitched by

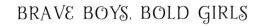

that wicked dwarf, who had stolen my treasure. At last he is dead and the spell has been broken."

Then everyone was full of joy. The girls took the treasure home to their mother. Soon, Snow-white married the prince and Rose-red married his brother. And they all lived peacefully and happily together for many years.

The Three Spinners

Long ago, there lived a very lazy girl. She would not sit and spin, no matter how much her mother asked her or coaxed her. Finally, her mother got so cross that she lost her temper. She gave her a good whack on the bottom and the shocked girl started crying loudly.

At that moment the queen was passing by. She heard the dreadful wailing and stopped to see what was going on.

The mother was too embarrassed to tell the queen about her daughter's terrible laziness, so she quickly made up a story.

"My daughter is crying because she loves spinning but she has run out of flax to spin with. I am very poor and she spins so much that I can't afford to buy enough flax to keep up with her!"

The queen replied: "In that case, your daughter shall come to the castle and live with me. I have plenty of flax – she can sit and spin there to her heart's content."

Of course, the mother was only too delighted to be rid of her lazy daughter – and the girl could not disobey the queen. So off she went to the castle. There, the queen showed her into a hallway with three rooms off it, each one filled to the ceiling with flax.

"Spin me all this flax and you can marry my eldest son," the queen told the girl. "I know you are poor, but that's not important to me. Just show me you are as hardworking as your mother says you are and you will be rewarded by marrying the prince." Then she went away and left the girl with a spinning wheel, to get on with it.

The girl sank down and wept bitterly.

It wasn't just that she hated spinning. She knew that it would take her a hundred years to spin that much flax. She sobbed till she could sob no more. Then she went to gaze sadly out of a window, wishing she were back at home, and that she had never been so lazy.

As she sat there crying, three old women walked by. The first of them had one really huge, wide, flat foot. The second had a massive bottom lip. And the third had one enormous, wide, flat thumb. They stopped in front of the window and one of them asked: "Why do you look so sad, my dear?"

The tearful girl explained and the three old women clucked comfortingly.

"We can help you," they offered. "We can spin all that flax in no time at all. Just promise to invite us to your wedding. You mustn't be ashamed of us – you must call us your cousins and let us sit at the high table with you."

The girl was delighted by their kind offer

and promised them all that they wanted.

So the women clambered in through the window and got spinning. The first one drew out the flax and used her huge, wide, flat foot to move the treddle that turned the wheel. The second one moistened the flax, sucking it over her massive bottom lip. And the third one twisted the flax then rapped on a table with her enormous, wide, flat thumb. Whenever she rapped, a heap of yarn fell to the ground, most beautifully spun.

The three women span for days and days. Whenever the queen came to check on the girl, the old ladies hid away. The girl showed the queen the spun yarn and she was absolutely thrilled. And so all the flax in the

first room was spun… then the second room… and then the third room.

Then the three old ladies clambered back out of the window, saying to the girl, "Don't forget what you have promised." And the girl showed the queen the empty rooms and the great heaps of yarn.

The wedding was arranged at once. The eldest prince was delighted to have such a clever and hardworking

163

bride and he fell in love with her the minute he saw her.

"I have three cousins," the girl told him, "and as they have always been extremely kind to me, I would like them to sit at the high table with us at the wedding."

"I don't see why not," he said.

So when the day of the wedding came, the three old women sat at the feast with the royal family.

The prince couldn't help remarking to his new bride, "How have you come to have such strange-looking relations?" And he went to the first old woman and asked: "How is it that you have such a huge, wide, flat foot?"

"From working at the spinning wheel,

treading flax," she answered.

Then he went to the second and said, "How is it that you have such a massive bottom lip?"

"From working at the spinning wheel, licking flax," she answered.

Then he asked the third, "How is it that you have such a wide, flat thumb?"

"From working at the spinning wheel, twisting flax," she answered.

From then on the prince never let his lovely wife work at a spinning wheel again.

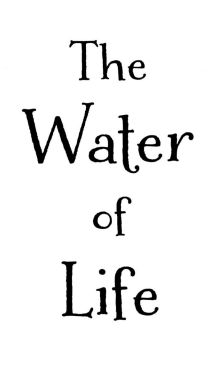

The Water of Life

Long ago, there was a king in a far-off country who fell ill and was dying. His three sons were dreadfully upset. One day, as the young men walked together sadly in the palace gardens, a little old man appeared.

"I know something that would save your father," he whispered to them, "the Water of Life." And he vanished just as suddenly as he had arrived.

Later that day, the eldest son jumped on his horse and went galloping away from the castle. He was off to find the Water of Life – but not only because he did not want his father to die. He also thought that if he was the one to save the king, the king would give all his kingdom to him, and he would not have to share it with his brothers.

When he had travelled some way he rode into a gloomy, wooded valley. There, standing on a rock, was an ugly little dwarf.

"Where are you going?" cried the dwarf.

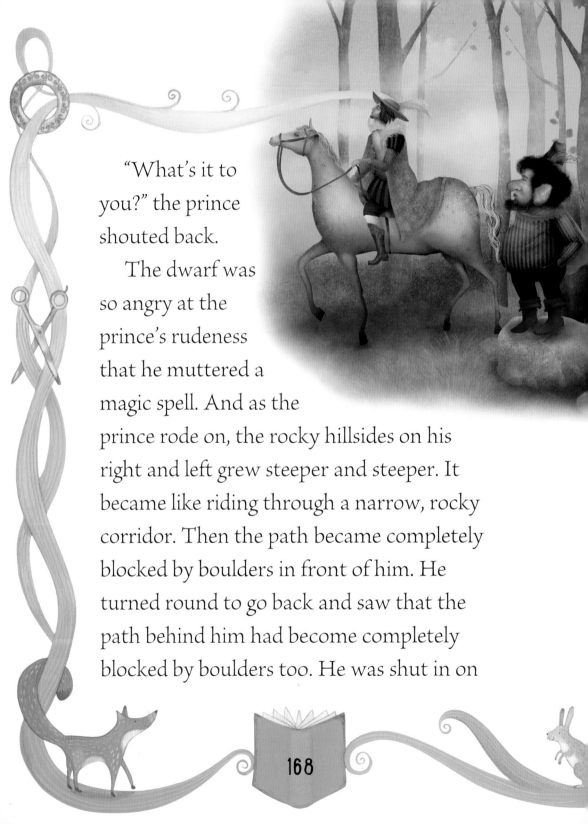

"What's it to you?" the prince shouted back.

The dwarf was so angry at the prince's rudeness that he muttered a magic spell. And as the prince rode on, the rocky hillsides on his right and left grew steeper and steeper. It became like riding through a narrow, rocky corridor. Then the path became completely blocked by boulders in front of him. He turned round to go back and saw that the path behind him had become completely blocked by boulders too. He was shut in on

all sides! The prince jumped off his horse and
discovered that he could not move a step – it
was as if his feet were glued to the floor. He
heard a loud laugh ringing through the air.
And he had to stay there, spellbound.

Days passed and the eldest prince did not
return to the palace, so the middle prince
thought he would try to find the Water of
Life. He too wanted to make his father better,
but also thought he might win the kingdom.

The middle prince followed the same road
as his elder brother. He also came across the
dwarf – and was just as rude! The dwarf put
the same spell on him and he also ended up
spellbound in a rocky prison.

When the second prince had been gone a

long time, the youngest prince set out to
search for the Water of Life. He wasn't
bothered about being given the whole
kingdom, he just wanted his father to be well.

He took the same road as his two brothers
and met the dwarf at the same spot. But
when the ugly little man called out, "Where
are you going so fast?" the prince replied:

"I am searching for the Water of Life
because my father is ill and going to die. But I
have no idea where to find it. Please, can you
help me?"

The dwarf was delighted that the prince
had spoken so politely and he said: "You will
find the Water of Life springing from a well
in an enchanted castle. Here is an iron wand

– when you reach the castle, hit the door three times with it and it will open. And here are two little loaves of bread – throw them to the lions waiting inside the door and they will not eat you up. Then hurry to fetch the Water of Life from the well. If the clock strikes twelve, the castle door will shut and you will be trapped there forever."

The prince thanked the dwarf many times and his new little friend showed him the road he should take to the enchanted castle.

After much hard riding, the prince arrived at the castle. Everything was as the dwarf had told him. At the third rap with the wand, the door flew open. When the lions were munching on the bread, he hurried on into

the depths of the castle,
looking for the well.

At last, the prince
finally found it,
standing in
one of the
castle's beautiful
courtyards. With
trembling hands, the
prince drew up a
bucket of the precious
Water of Life and poured it into
a golden cup that stood at the edge of the
well. Just then the clock began to strike…

One! Two! Three! The prince dashed back
through the courtyards…

Four! Five! Six! He sped through the castle...

Seven! Eight! Nine! He raced past the lions.

Ten! Eleven! He reached the castle door and leapt through.

Twelve! He heard the heavy door clang shut behind him forever. Phew! The prince was safe – and overjoyed to think that he had got the Water of Life.

He got back on his horse and set off home at a gallop. On the way, he passed the dwarf once more. The prince thanked him heartily for his help and said: "My dear friend, are you

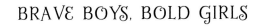

able to tell me where my lost brothers are?"

The dwarf explained what had happened. Then he said, "They have learned their lesson – they will not be rude again," and he kindly returned the prince's brothers to him.

All three young men rode home together. The youngest son gave his father the Water of Life to drink and the king became well again. He arranged a splendid feast to celebrate his miraculous recovery – and of course the ugly little dwarf was the most important guest.

The Rabbit's Bride

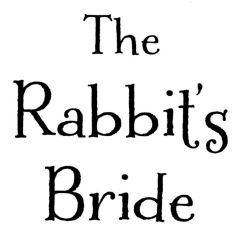

There was once a woman who lived with her grown-up daughter in a little cottage. They had a vegetable patch where they grew prize cabbages. But one day a rabbit came and began to eat them all up.

The woman was annoyed and said to her daughter: "Get rid of that pesky rabbit!"

So the girl ran down the garden to the cabbage patch crying: "Shoo! Shoo! Don't you dare eat up all our cabbages, Mr Rabbit!"

To her surprise, the rabbit didn't scamper away. It turned and spoke to her. "My dear,"

it said, twitching its fine long whiskers, "come and live with me in my burrow."

"Well I never!" said the girl, most put out. The rabbit shrugged and leapt away. The girl stomped back to the cottage.

The next day, the rabbit came back. And again the girl ran to the cabbage patch crying: "Shoo! Shoo! Don't you dare eat up all our cabbages, Mr Rabbit!"

"Well, have you thought about what I said?" the rabbit said, wiggling his soft tail at her cheekily. "Will you come and live with me in my burrow?"

"Certainly not!" said the girl, in a huff. The rabbit just shrugged and leapt away, and the girl strode back angrily to the cottage.

The following day, there was the rabbit again. And for the third time, the girl ran to the cabbage patch crying: "Shoo! Shoo! Don't you dare eat up all our cabbages, Mr Rabbit!"

"So," said the rabbit, winking at her, "are you going to come and live with me in my burrow or not?"

Suddenly, the girl had an idea. "All right," she said.

The rabbit beamed. "Hop on to my tail and I'll take you there," he said. So the girl did so and away they went.

When they reached the burrow, the rabbit let the girl down from his tail and said: "Now, you get to work and prepare a feast. I am going to tell all my family and friends the good news, and invite them to the wedding."

So the girl began to cook and the rabbit scuttled away and left her on her own.

As soon as the rabbit had gone, the girl took some straw and tied it with twine to make a figure about the same size and shape as herself. Then she dressed it in her own clothes. Next, she painted a face on it. Finally, she sat the figure in front of the oven so that it looked like it was keeping an eye on the cooking, and then she ran all the way home to her mother.

After a while the rabbit returned to the burrow. "Hello my dear," he said, "how are you getting on with everything?" and he went over and put his paw around the straw figure, which he thought was the girl. But as he touched it the figure's head fell off and rolled away across the kitchen floor!

"Oh my goodness!" gasped the rabbit, quite horrified. "I've killed her!"

And he scampered away, as fast as his legs could leap.

I have heard tell that the rabbit settled in a new home far away and found a lovely lady rabbit who was very happy to be his wife – but that may only be gossip. One thing's for sure: the woman, the girl and their cabbages were never bothered by rabbits again.

Tom Thumb

There was once a poor woodcutter and his wife who had a teeny-tiny baby boy who grew up to be no bigger than a thumb. Small as he was, the couple loved him dearly. Tom was good and thoughtful and

helped his parents as best he could.

One morning, as usual, the woodcutter went into the forest to cut down firewood. Tom's mother harnessed the horse to the cart which the woodcutter would need to fetch the cut logs. Then she lifted little Tom into the horse's ear. "Giddy up!" Tom squeaked, and the animal lumbered forwards. And so Tom drove the horse down the path towards his father in the wood, shouting directions into the animal's ear all the way.

But it so happened that two strangers saw the horse as it pulled the cart through the trees. "How very strange!" one said to the other. "I can see a cart going along, and I can hear a voice calling out to the horse, but I

can't see anyone!" They followed behind until they reached the place where the woodcutter was. They saw the woodcutter take tiny Tom Thumb down from the horse's ear and sit him on a straw, where he perched merrily.

"Can you see that? It's incredible!" one stranger remarked.

"Yes, and just think – if we had that tiny boy, we could show him off for money and make our fortune," said the other, craftily.

So the strangers went up to the woodcutter and asked him what price he would take for the little man.

"Sell him?" cried the woodcutter, quite horrified. "Of course I won't – he's my son!"

But Tom Thumb crept up his father's coat

onto his shoulder and whispered in his ear: "I have an idea, Father. Sell me for as much money as you can. Don't worry – I'll come back to you, I promise."

So the woodcutter trusted his tiny boy and sold him to the strangers for a whole bag of gold pieces. Tom Thumb said a cheery goodbye to his father and hopped up on to one of the stranger's hats, and off they went travelling down the road.

The strangers walked till the sun was high in the sky. Then Tom said: "Let me get down for a bit to stretch my legs." So the man took off his hat and put Tom down by the side of the road – and he instantly ran off out of sight. The strangers searched and searched, but they could not find Tom, for he had disappeared down a mousehole. So they were forced to go on their way without him, sulky as can be.

As soon as Tom saw they were gone, he came out of his hiding place. He set off back down the road until darkness began to fall. Then he came across an empty snail-shell. "This is lucky," he said, "I can sleep here very well." And in he crept.

Bright and early next morning, Tom set off towards home once more. But alas, he didn't hear a wolf creeping up on him from behind – till it was too

late and he had been swallowed in one gulp!

From inside the wolf's stomach, Tom felt the animal start to run in great bounds. He thought hard and quickly came up with a plan. "My friend," he called out, as loud as he could. "I know where more tasty treats are to be found."

The wolf was most surprised that something in his stomach was speaking to him, but he was very curious. "Tell me more, whoever you are," he replied.

So Tom described his parents' cottage and where it was. "When you find it, you can crawl through the drain into the kitchen, and then into the pantry," he suggested. "There you will find ham, beef, cold chicken, roast pig, cakes, apple cider, and everything that your heart can wish." For Tom was sure that the pantry would be well-stocked, now his parents had the bag of gold.

The wolf did not need to be told twice. He sped away to the woodcutter's cottage and, that night, when Tom's parents had gone to bed and the house was dark and still, he crawled through the drain into the kitchen and into the pantry. There he ate and drank to his heart's content. Then he tried to squeeze out the way he had squeezed in. But he found that his stomach was now so big and full that he just would not fit, no matter how hard he tried.

That was just what Tom had counted on

and now he began to shout at the top of his voice: "Father! Mother! It's me, Tom! I'm inside the wolf in the pantry."

"Will you shut up?" snarled the wolf. He leapt about in a panic and in doing so he made such a clatter knocking jars and bottles off the shelves that he made even more noise than Tom.

The woodcutter and his wife woke and went down to the pantry to see whatever was causing the commotion. They peeped through a crack in the door and saw the wolf bounding about. But the woodcutter was not afraid. He was overjoyed to hear his son's tiny voice crying out: "Father! Mother! I am here – the wolf has swallowed me!"

Then the woodcutter took his axe and counted: "Three… two… one!" On the last count, his wife flung the pantry door open wide and – *BOP!* The woodcutter bashed the wolf on the head with the handle of the axe and the creature fell down, dead. The woodcutter carefully cut open the animal's body – and out jumped Tom Thumb, alive and well!

Then the woodcutter and his wife hugged and kissed their tiny boy and promised they would never be parted again. They gave him plenty to eat and drink, and dressed him in smart new clothes – for now they did not have to worry about money. And Tom Thumb was quite happy to never leave his

parents again. He felt he had seen quite enough of the world and had decided there was no place like home!

The Iron Stove

In the days when wishing was still of some use, a king's son was enchanted by an old witch and shut up in an iron stove in a forest. Many years went by and no one came along to break the spell to set him free. Then, at long last, a princess came wandering by. She was most alarmed to hear a voice crying from inside the stove. "Help! Please help me!" it said. Bravely she went closer. "Who are you?" the voice asked her.

"I am a princess," the young woman explained, "but I have got lost in this forest and can't find my way back home."

"I am an enchanted prince," the voice from inside the stove replied. "I will tell you how to get home, if you promise to do what I ask to break the spell and set me free."

"Of course I will," promised the princess.

So the prince told the princess that she needed to come back with a knife and scrape a hole in the iron. Then he gave her directions to get back to her kingdom and she ran off through the trees.

When the princess finally returned to her castle, her father, the king, rejoiced. His wife had died long ago and the princess was his only child – he had thought he had lost her as well! "I would never have found my way home at all," the princess explained, "if I hadn't come across an enchanted prince in an iron stove. I have given my word that I will go back and set him free."

The king was very fearful that something else might happen to his dear daughter if she returned to the wood, but the princess insisted. "I must keep my word," she said, and she put a knife into her pocket and set off

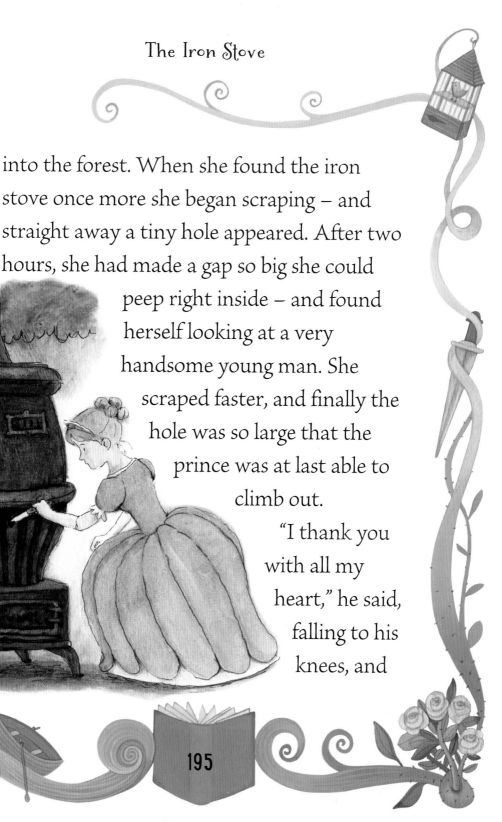

into the forest. When she found the iron
stove once more she began scraping – and
straight away a tiny hole appeared. After two
hours, she had made a gap so big she could
peep right inside – and found
herself looking at a very
handsome young man. She
scraped faster, and finally the
hole was so large that the
prince was at last able to
climb out.

"I thank you
with all my
heart," he said,
falling to his
knees, and

asking the princess to marry him. She was delighted and said yes.

But before travelling with him to live in his kingdom, she asked if she could be allowed to go and say goodbye to her father. "Very well," agreed the prince, "but be warned – you must not speak more than three words."

The princess thought this was rather strange, but she kissed the prince, promised she would remember, and hurried back home to her father.

Of course she forgot her promise. She spoke far more than three words when telling her father all about the handsome prince and how she had agreed to marry him and go to his kingdom. As she talked, a magic wind

blew through the forest and wiped every memory of her from her beloved prince's head. Then it swept him off his feet and carried him back to his own kingdom.

Next day, when the princess returned to the forest, her sweetheart was nowhere to be found. She searched for days, growing more and more exhausted and hungry, but there was no sign of him.

Finally, the princess stumbled across a little cottage, overgrown with grass and moss. She peeped inside a window and saw several toads sitting at a table, eating a fine dinner. She knocked at the door and the smallest toad opened it and invited her to sit and eat with them.

The princess told the kind creatures
everything that had happened and, to her
delight, the biggest toad said they could help
her. Then they presented her with a nut,
which they told her to take great care of and
open when she needed help, and took her to

the path through the forest which led to the prince's castle.

The brave princess had to cross a high glass mountain, a field that grew plants as sharp as swords, and a lake as wide as the sea. But, finally, she reached her sweetheart's castle. However, by now her clothes were ragged and tattered and she looked quite unlike the princess she really was. How would she ever be allowed to enter the court and see the prince? She sank down against the castle wall and sobbed.

Suddenly, the princess felt something small and hard in her pocket – and pulled out the nut. She cracked it with her teeth and opened it – and inside was the most beautiful

dress, edged in fine lace and pearls.

Overjoyed, the princess put it on – of course it fitted perfectly – and knocked at the castle door. When the servants saw how fine she looked they welcomed her in at once. As soon as the prince laid his eyes on her, he remembered her, and leapt up and kissed her.

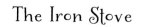

From that day on, the two were never parted. They even sent for the princess's father, the old king, so he would not have to live on his own. And together, they all lived happily for many years.

The Twelve Dancing Princesses

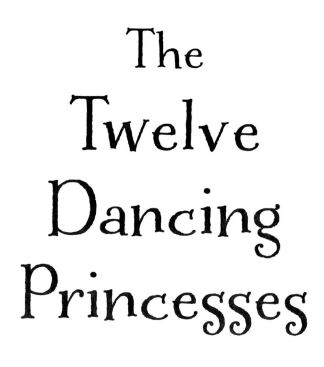

Once upon a time, there was a king who had twelve beautiful daughters. Each night, they settled down to sleep in their bedroom and the king locked the door, to keep them safe. But then something very strange would happen. In the morning, the princesses' shoes all had holes worn in the soles, just as if they had been danced in all night.

Neither the king, nor his wisest advisors, had any idea how it happened. But morning, after morning, after morning, it was the same – there were twelve worn-out pairs of shoes by the twelve beds. At last, the king sent messengers throughout the land to announce that if anyone could discover what was going on, he could marry whichever princess he liked best. But anyone who tried and failed would be thrown out of the kingdom, never to return.

Well, many princes and dukes and earls

and knights came from far and wide to try
their luck. Each night, one of them was
locked into the princesses' room, determined
to stay awake and watch and find out what
happened. But each night, the young man fell
asleep. In the morning, there were twelve
pairs of worn-out shoes and the young man
was none the wiser. By the afternoon, he had
been banished from the land forever.

Time passed, until hardly any young men
arrived any more to find out what was
happening to the shoes. But then a soldier
came wandering into the kingdom, on his
way home from battle. He came across an old
woman on the road and offered to carry her
heavy basket for her. The old woman was

very pleased and told him about the chance to win one of the princesses as his wife.

"Listen carefully," she said. "In the evening, one of the princesses will bring you a goblet of wine. Just pretend to drink it, then make it look as though you are fast asleep." She brought out a cloak from her basket and gave it to him, saying: "Whenever you put this on, you will become invisible. You will be able to watch what the princesses do without them seeing you."

The soldier thanked the old woman many times and set off to the castle. There, he was welcomed very warmly. In the evening, he was shown into the princesses' bedroom and the king locked the door.

Just as the old woman had said, one of the beautiful girls brought the soldier a goblet of wine. The soldier remembered what he had to do and he threw it away when the princess wasn't looking. Then he lay down on a sofa and pretended to snore.

The twelve princesses giggled. Then, instead of getting into their beds, they took off their pyjamas and put on their finest dresses and their shoes.

Next, the eldest princess went to her bed and clapped her hands. Her bed flew up to the ceiling and a trap-door that was underneath sprang open. The princesses skipped happily down, one after the other.

When the room was empty, the soldier jumped up and put on the cloak the old woman had given him. He marvelled at himself in one of the room's many mirrors – he was quite invisible, just as the old woman had said he would be. Then, quickly and quietly, he followed the girls down through the trap-door. He found himself descending a steep, lamp-lit staircase.

At the bottom, he came out into daylight, where a beautiful silver lake sparkled under a

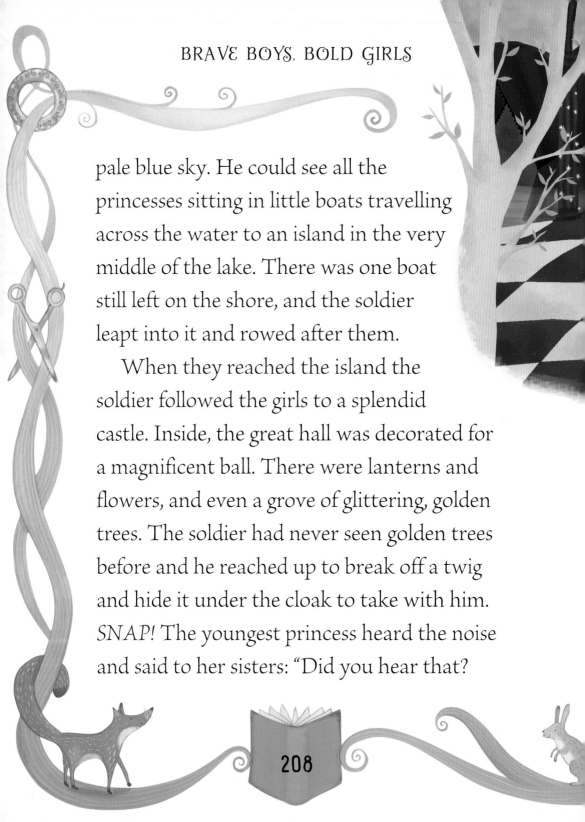

pale blue sky. He could see all the princesses sitting in little boats travelling across the water to an island in the very middle of the lake. There was one boat still left on the shore, and the soldier leapt into it and rowed after them.

When they reached the island the soldier followed the girls to a splendid castle. Inside, the great hall was decorated for a magnificent ball. There were lanterns and flowers, and even a grove of glittering, golden trees. The soldier had never seen golden trees before and he reached up to break off a twig and hide it under the cloak to take with him. *SNAP!* The youngest princess heard the noise and said to her sisters: "Did you hear that?

What was it? Do you think someone is here with us?"

But the eldest princess said, "Don't be silly, of course not!" And she set off into the hall, leaving her sisters to follow.

The princesses joined the guests having a wonderful time there, and they danced and danced and danced. The soldier danced invisibly with them too!

By three o'clock in the morning, the princesses had danced so much that their shoes were quite worn out, so they had to stop. They said a joyful but weary goodbye to the other guests, promising to come back again the next night.

Then the soldier had seen enough. He knew he had to keep his wits about him or he would not reach the princesses' bedroom before they did. As the princesses were putting on their capes and hats ready for the return journey, he ran swiftly from the castle and back to the lake. Then he rowed as hard as he could back across the lake and ran at full pelt to the stairs.

By the time the princesses had climbed

back up to their bedroom he was lying just where they had left him on the sofa, seemingly fast asleep.

Of course the next morning the princesses' shoes were inspected and once more they were full of holes and quite worn out. The soldier was shown before the king, and the twelve princesses stood listening behind the door to hear what he was going to say.

But when the king asked the soldier with a weary voice: "So, why are my daughters' shoes worn out each morning?" the soldier did not mumble and stutter, like all the other young men had done. Instead he told the unlikely tale of how the princesses had danced all night.

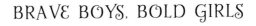

The king glowered at the soldier – he thought the whole story sounded highly unlikely. He was about to accuse him of making the whole thing up, when the soldier pulled out the golden twig and offered it as proof of his adventure!

The king examined the twig carefully – it sparkled and twinkled at him in the early morning light. He had never seen anything of its kind before.

He called for the princesses, who were astonished at the soldier knowing their secret. They told their father the truth at once. Then the king asked the soldier which of the princesses he would choose for his wife. Of course, he chose the youngest – for she was the one who had nearly guessed he was there. And after they were married, he made sure he danced with her and her sisters every day.

FAERY FOLK

Rumpelstiltskin

Once upon a time, there lived a
miller and his daughter. They were
very poor and the people round about looked
down on them. So one day the miller told a
terrible fib about his daughter, to make them

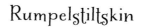

seem more important. "My daughter knows how to spin straw into gold!" he boasted.

The news spread and soon reached the king – and he was most excited. "I want to see this for myself!" he exclaimed. "Have the girl brought to my palace tomorrow!"

The miller's daughter could not disobey so, very nervously, she presented herself at the palace. To her horror, the king showed her to a room piled with straw to the ceiling. He gave her a spinning wheel and said: "If you haven't spun this straw into gold by tomorrow morning, you will die." He went out of the room and locked her in, all alone.

Now, the miller's daughter was beautiful – and clever too – but she had no idea how to

spin straw into gold. She began to weep.

All at once the door creaked open and in came a strange little man. "Good morning, Miss," he said. "What are you crying about?"

"I have to spin straw into gold – and I don't have a clue how to do it," the miller's daughter sobbed.

"What will you give me if I do it for you?" asked the little man.

The miller's daughter thought fast. "My bracelet!" she cried.

The little man took the bracelet. Then he sat at the spinning wheel and – *whirr, whirr, whirr!* – he span all day and late into the night. Finally all the straw was gone – and reels of pure gold covered the floor! Then the

little man strode out and the door locked itself behind him.

At daybreak the king arrived. When he saw the gold he was astonished and delighted! But he was greedy. He took the miller's daughter to another room. It was even larger – and it too was piled with straw to the ceiling. "Now let's see you do it again," the king said. "If you can't, you will die." And he went out and locked the door.

Once again, the girl sank down and began to cry, when the door opened and there was the strange little man.

"What will you give me if I help you again?" he asked.

"The ring on my finger," the girl offered.

The little man grinned and took the ring, sat at the spinning wheel once more, and by midnight all the straw had been turned into reels of glittering gold.

At daybreak the king arrived. How thrilled he was! But he took the miller's daughter into an even bigger room, filled with even more straw. This time he said: "Spin all this straw into gold by morning and I will make you my wife! But fail – and you will die." And off he went.

The miller's daughter despaired. Surely the strange little man wouldn't appear and help her a third time. But so he did! The door opened and he sauntered in, asking: "What will you give me this time?"

The miller's daughter hung her head. "I have nothing left," she said, hopelessly.

Then the little man's eyes glinted. "Promise me," he said, "that when you become queen, you will give me your first-born child."

The miller's daughter had no choice. If she did not promise what the little man wanted, she would die. With a heavy heart, she said: "I promise," and the little man sat down and span all the straw into gold.

Next morning, when the king arrived, he could not believe his eyes. He kissed the miller's daughter, and the following day he married her.

The queen found her new life with the

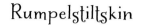

king very exciting. After about a year, she gave birth to a beautiful child and her happiness was complete – until the strange little man suddenly appeared. "Give me what you promised," he demanded.

The queen had forgotten all about him, and she was horrified. "No!" she gasped. "I will give you all the riches in the kingdom, but please – I cannot give you my baby!"

"I already have enough riches," the little man said, shaking his head. "I want the child."

Then the queen began to weep – so heartbreakingly that the little man took pity on her. "I will give you three days," he said. "If you can guess my name when I return, you can keep your baby." And he disappeared just

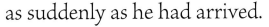

as suddenly as he had arrived.

All night, the queen thought frantically of every name she had ever heard. The next day, when the little man appeared, she ran through her whole list: "Is it Caspar?… Melchior?… Balthazar?…" and so on.

But the little man just answered: "That is not my name," to each one. And when the queen had read out every name, he giggled and disappeared.

Straight away, the queen sent out messengers to search for other names. So the next day, when the little man appeared again, she had another list. "Perhaps your name is Shortribs?" she asked. "Or Sheepshanks?… Or Laceleg?…" and so on.

But the little man just answered: "That is not my name," to each one. When the queen had run out, he laughed and vanished. The queen wrung her hands and wept.

Late that evening a messenger returned to the palace and told her: "I travelled until I came to a mountain where there was a little house. A campfire was burning outside, and round the campfire danced the strangest little man I have ever seen. He was singing a strange song. It went: 'I'll win the game! For no one can guess that Rumpelstiltskin is my name!'"

The queen was overjoyed with the messenger's news. When the strange little man appeared on the third morning, she was quite calm and ready.

"Is your name…" she pretended to wonder. "Might it possibly be… Is there any chance at all that you could be called… *Rumpelstiltskin?*"

"SOMEONE TOLD YOU!" roared the little man, hopping up and down, totally enraged. "WHO TOLD YOU?"

But the queen refused to tell, and in his anger Rumpelstiltskin jumped up and down

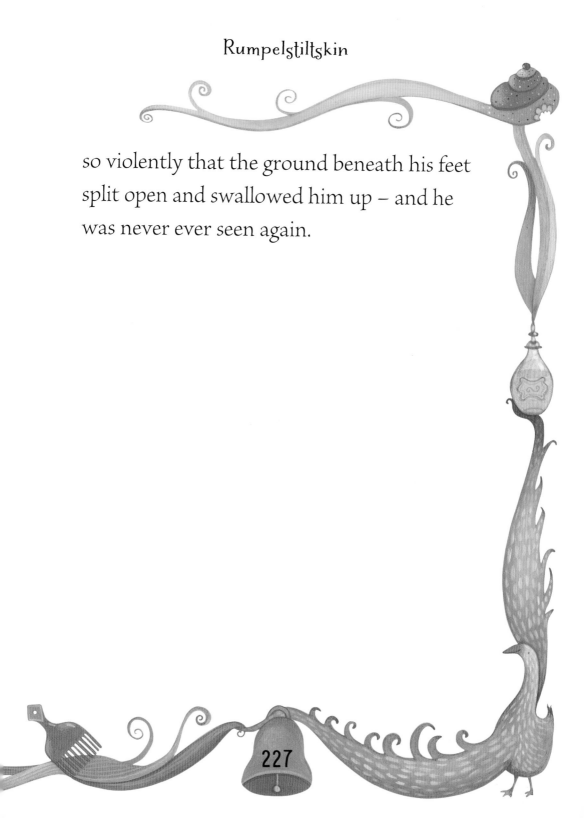

so violently that the ground beneath his feet split open and swallowed him up – and he was never ever seen again.

The Water Nix

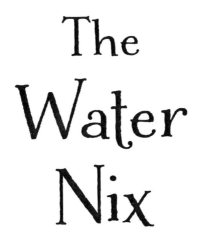

One day long ago, in a land far away, a little brother and sister were playing by a well. They ran about in the sunshine, happily chasing each other, until the little girl tripped. Over she toppled, into

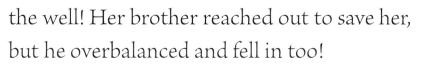

the well! Her brother reached out to save her, but he overbalanced and fell in too!

Unfortunately, a mischievous water sprite called a nix lived down below. She was delighted to see the two children come splashing into the water and she grabbed them, saying: "Got you! Now you will live with me and do all my hard work." And the water nix pulled them down to the bottom of the well.

The children were astonished to see that the world at the bottom of the well was very similar to the world above that they had left. The water nix dragged them off to her house and set them to work. The little boy had to chop down trees for firewood – with a blunt

axe! The little girl had to sit at a spinning wheel and spin tangled, dirty flax.

Then they had to fetch water for the cottage – but the buckets the nix gave them had holes in them! All the nix gave the children to eat was dumplings as hard as stones. How miserable the children were! They were tired and

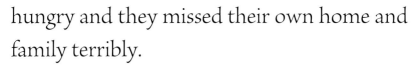

hungry and they missed their own home and family terribly.

At last a chance came for the children to escape. One Sunday the water nix put on her best clothes and went to see a friend. As soon as she was over the hill and out of sight the two children took each other by the hand and ran off, as fast as their little legs would carry them.

When the nix returned from her visit and found her servants gone, she was furious! She growled and gnashed her teeth, and set off after them with huge, long strides.

The little boy and girl felt the earth begin to shake and as they ran they looked behind them. The water nix was coming!

Quick as lightning, the little girl took her hairbrush from her pocket and threw it behind her. While the children kept running, the hairbrush grew and grew – until it was a hill covered in sharp spikes that blocked the water nix's path.

The water nix roared with rage. Slowly, she scrambled all the way up and over the hill, and although the thousands of sharp spikes stabbed her a million times, she did not stop…

The children could once more hear the water nix gaining on them, yelling and cursing all the time. Then the little boy took his comb from his pocket and threw it back over his shoulder.

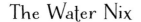

While they kept running, the comb grew and grew – until it became a steep cliff covered in a forest of deadly spears.

The water nix howled and bellowed with fury. Very slowly, she crawled over and around and through the spears, and although they jabbed her painfully on all sides, she still did not stop…

The wind blew her hot panting breath onto the back of the children's necks. They glanced behind and saw the nix closing in on them. The children thrust their hands in their pockets – all they had left was the little girl's pocket mirror. The little girl threw it behind her as far as she could. While the children kept running, the pocket mirror

grew and grew – until it was a
mountain made entirely of
glass. It was so slippery that it
was impossible for the nix to
cross it! All she could
do was go home to
fetch her axe, so she
could come back
and chop the glass
mountain to bits.

But the children
kept running…
and when the
water nix finally
returned and
demolished the

glass mountain, they were long gone. How the nix growled and gnashed her teeth!

The little boy and girl found their way back home. And there they lived happily ever after – unlike the water nix, who had only her wicked self for company.

The Young Giant

Once upon a time there lived a farmer and his wife. The couple had a son who was no bigger than the farmer's thumb. One day, father and son were out working in the fields when an old giant came

stomping over the hill. He bent down and scooped up Tiny Tom, turned him round, carefully examining him, and then strode off with him without a word. The farmer was horrified – but he could do nothing to stop the giant. He sank down on the earth, broken-hearted, thinking he would never see his little son again.

The old giant did not harm Tiny Tom, however. Quite the opposite. He took him back to his own house and fed him and cared for him well. Time passed and Tiny Tom grew much taller and stronger. After two years had gone by, he had become the size of a young giant.

The old giant was delighted. He decided to

take Tiny Tom into the forest, to see what he could do.

"Pull up a stick for yourself," he said.

The boy was so strong that he tore a young tree out of the ground, roots and all!

But the old giant thought: 'I'm sure I can make him better than that.'

So he cared for Tiny Tom for two more years and then took him into the forest again.

By this time, the lad had become so much taller and stronger that he could rip a huge old tree out of the ground.

'Hmmm,' thought the old giant. 'I'm sure I can make him even better.'

So he looked after Tiny Tom for a further two years and then took him into the forest

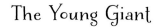

once more. "Now pull up a proper stick for me," he said. And the young man tore up the strongest oak tree in all the forest.

Then the old giant beamed. "Perfect!" he said, and he showed Tiny Tom the way back to the field he had found him in, six years ago.

Tiny Tom's father was working there as usual, ploughing the soil. He was terrified when he saw the young giant striding towards him.

"Hello father," the young man boomed. "Look what a fine fellow I've grown into!"

"You're not my son!" the farmer replied. "You can't be!"

"But I am," the young giant insisted. "You go home and I'll plough the field for you. Tell

mother to cook supper for me – I'll be back
to see her shortly."

So Tiny Tom's father went off, shaking his
head and muttering to himself, while Tiny
Tom unhitched the horses, harnessed himself
to the plough, and ploughed the field in five
minutes flat. Then he strode off home.

"Who's that horrible tall man?" Tiny
Tom's mother whispered to his father, as he
paced into the farmyard.

"He says he is our son," Tiny Tom's father
whispered back.

"How can he be?" cried his mother. "Our
son was just a tiny little thing!"

She brought him two massive dishes full of
food – enough to feed her and her husband

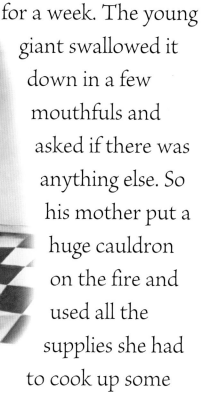

for a week. The young giant swallowed it down in a few mouthfuls and asked if there was anything else. So his mother put a huge cauldron on the fire and used all the supplies she had to cook up some stew. The young giant gulped it back and asked: "What else have you got, Mother?"

"Nothing," she replied crossly, "that's all we have."

"But I'm still hungry," the mighty man grumbled. Then he realized that he had grown too big to live at home any more. "Father," he said, "I see that if I stay here I'll eat you out of house and home, and that will not do. I will have to go out into the world and seek my fortune."

The next day, the young giant said goodbye to his parents, took the thickest iron bar he could find to use as a staff, and set off down the road.

Tiny Tom travelled over hill and dale and eventually came to a small farm where the farmer was looking for a chief worker. The young giant offered his services and the farmer and his wife were delighted at the

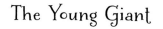

thought of having such a huge, strong man working for them. "How much do you want as pay?" the farmer asked. To his great astonishment, the giant replied: "Nothing… only after I have worked for you for a year, let me hit you two times."

The farmer and his wife thought the strange bargain was some sort of joke. "Very well," they agreed, laughing, and thought no more of it.

Next day, Tiny Tom started work. Early in the morning, all the farmhands started getting ready to go into the woods to chop trees. "Get up!" they told the young giant. "You are our new chief and you're still lying in bed."

But he just said, "Do as you like. I shall get the work done quicker than any of you."

The other workers set off into the forest and Tiny Tom stayed in bed for another four hours. Then he got up, and slowly ate a huge breakfast, and a while later he consumed a massive lunch. Only then did he stomp off after the other workers into the forest.

He met them as they were on their way home for the day, leading horses which pulled carts that were full of the logs they had cut. But the young giant wasn't worried. He just ripped the trees out of the earth, tossed them like matchsticks

into a cart and pulled it back to the farm
much faster than any horse could go,
overtaking the other workers on the way.

Of course the farmer was very pleased
with Tiny Tom's first day of work. "Look," he
said to his wife, "even if he spends most of the

day asleep, he still finishes his work before all the others."

So Tiny Tom served the farmer for a whole year – and then, when the other workers were getting their wages, it was time for him to have his two hits.

"Stand still," he said to the farmer. The farmer smirked and did as he was told, and the young giant hit him with such great force that the farmer flew up into the air and didn't come down.

"WHAT—" the farmer's wife began to shout at Tiny Tom in shock, but before she could finish, the young giant took the second part of his payment and hit her up into the sky too.

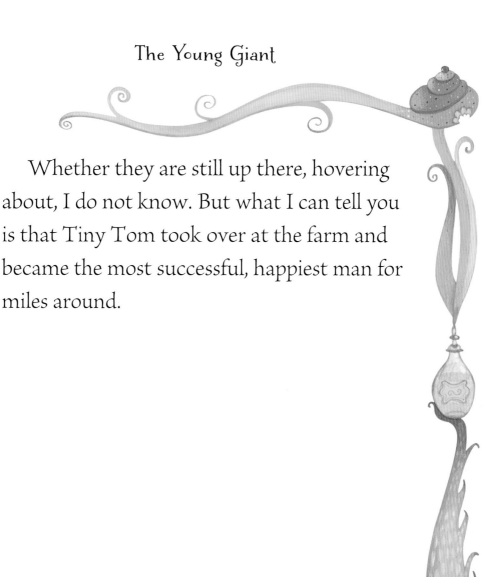

Whether they are still up there, hovering about, I do not know. But what I can tell you is that Tiny Tom took over at the farm and became the most successful, happiest man for miles around.

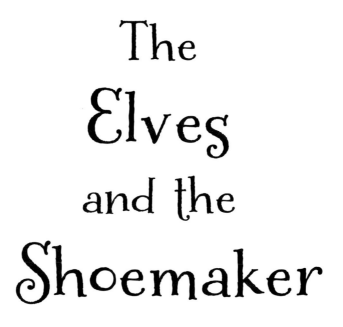

The Elves and the Shoemaker

Once upon a time, there lived a
shoemaker who became very poor. At
last he only had enough leather left to make
one more pair of shoes. That evening, he sat
sadly at his workbench, drew the shapes for

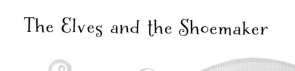

the shoes, and cut them out. "I'll sew these together in the morning," he sighed. "Once they're made and sold, heaven knows what will happen to me." And he shuffled off to bed.

Next morning, the shoemaker went back to his workbench, and was amazed to see the two shoes quite finished on his table. He blinked, and rubbed his eyes, and pinched himself – but he wasn't dreaming, they were still there. The shoemaker was totally flabbergasted.

He reached out nervously and picked up
the shoes. Very carefully, he turned them
over in his hands. They were so neatly made
that he could hardly see the stitches! They
were the most beautiful pair of shoes that he
had ever seen! The shoemaker sighed and
scratched his head. Then he put the shoes in
his window and opened up the shop, feeling
totally bewildered.

He didn't have long to wait before a
customer came in, eager to buy the shoes.
The woman paid the shoemaker a very good
price. The shoemaker couldn't believe his
luck. Now he had the money to buy enough
leather for two more pairs of shoes!

That night, he sat at his workbench

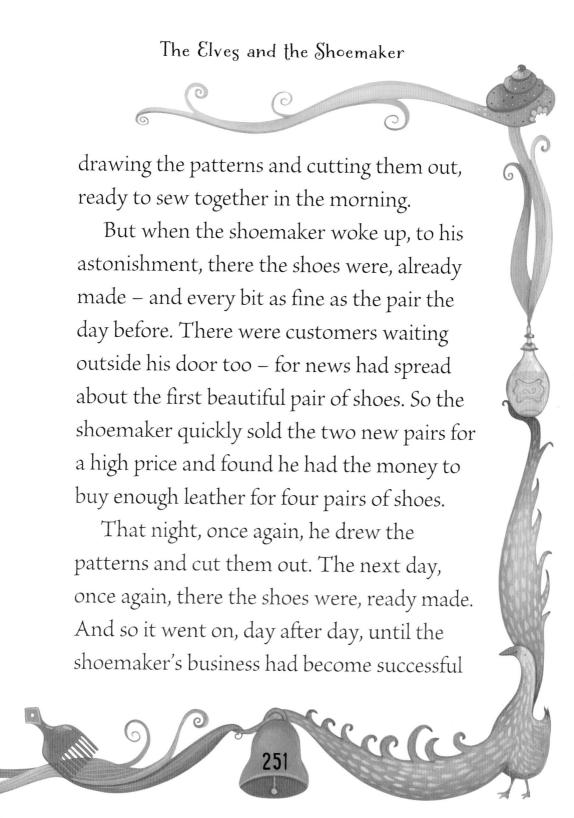

drawing the patterns and cutting them out, ready to sew together in the morning.

But when the shoemaker woke up, to his astonishment, there the shoes were, already made – and every bit as fine as the pair the day before. There were customers waiting outside his door too – for news had spread about the first beautiful pair of shoes. So the shoemaker quickly sold the two new pairs for a high price and found he had the money to buy enough leather for four pairs of shoes.

That night, once again, he drew the patterns and cut them out. The next day, once again, there the shoes were, ready made. And so it went on, day after day, until the shoemaker's business had become successful

once again and he had become a rich man.

One evening, the shoemaker said to his wife, "Why don't we stay up tonight and see if we can spot who comes and helps us?"

The shoemaker's wife thought it was a great idea. They left a candle burning in the workshop and hid behind a curtain.

They peeped out and waited, and at midnight two teeny-tiny men crept into the workshop. They were smaller than the shoemaker's little finger and wore simple, raggedy clothes and caps. They sat down at the shoemaker's workbench, picked up all the leather which was laid out, and began to stitch, and sew, and hammer. They were so skilful and quick that the shoemaker and his

wife couldn't take their eyes off them. The little men didn't stop until all the leather was stitched into beautiful shoes. Then away they ran into the night.

The next morning the shoemaker's wife said, "Those little men have made us rich, and we really must thank them for it. Did you notice how tatty their clothes were? I'll tell you what we should do: I'll sew them new little shirts, and coats, and vests, and trousers, and you make them two tiny pairs of shoes."

So that is what they did.

A few nights later, when everything was ready, they laid their presents out on the workbench and hid behind the curtain.

At midnight, the teeny-tiny men came

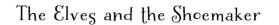

creeping in as usual – and how happy they
were to find their new outfits! They hurried
to put them on at once, then they danced
about with glee.

Then the two little men skipped away into
the night… and the shoemaker and his wife
never saw them again. But they didn't need
them anyway, because from then on, they
always seemed to have good luck in all that
they did.

Mother Holle

There was once a widow who had a daughter and a stepdaughter. Her daughter was ugly and lazy, while her stepdaughter was pretty and hard-working. However, the woman loved her own

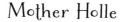

daughter more. She was cruel to her stepdaughter and made her do all the hardest jobs around the house, while her daughter took it easy.

One day, the stepdaughter was made to work at a spinning wheel until her fingers bled! A drop of blood fell on to the shuttle, and the girl hurried to the well to wash it off. As she dipped the shuttle in the water, it slipped from her hand and fell to the bottom.

How frightened the girl was! She didn't dare return home without the shuttle for she knew her stepmother would beat her. She also knew she might die if she jumped into the well to try to fetch it – but she decided that this was what she must do.

She took a deep breath, and jumped in.

Down... down... down... the stepdaughter sank into the well. Everything around her went black and she fainted.

When she came to, she was lying in a sunny meadow. She picked herself up and set off, walking.

After a while, she came to a bakery, where the oven was full of bread. The bread cried out to her, "Oh, take

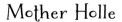

me out or I shall burn!" So the stepdaughter hurried to rescue the loaves.

She went on till she came to a tree covered with apples. The tree called out to her, "Oh shake me, my apples are all ripe!" So the girl shook the tree till the apples fell like rain. She gathered them into a neat heap and went on her way.

Then she came to a little house where an old woman sat outside. The old woman had such large teeth that the girl was frightened, and was about to run away. But the old woman called out to her, "Don't be afraid, dear child. Stay with me and if you do all the work in the house properly, you will be rewarded. The most important thing is

– when you make my bed, shake the quilt and pillows out so thoroughly that the feathers fly everywhere, for then there is snow on Earth."

The old woman seemed to be very kind, so the girl took courage and agreed to stay with her. She worked hard and every day she remembered to shake the quilt and pillows so hard that the feathers flew about like snowflakes. The old woman, whose name was Mother Holle, was always nice to her and made sure she was comfortable.

Time passed. The girl was happier with Mother Holle than she had been with her stepmother, but she still missed her home.

Mother Holle understood. "Of course you

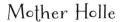

miss home, my dear," she said. "I will take you there myself."

She led the girl to a large door, and as the girl walked through the doorway, a shower of gold pieces fell on her. They stuck all over, so she was completely covered with gold! "That is your reward for working so hard," Mother Holle explained. She handed the girl the shuttle that had fallen into the well and the door swung shut.

To the girl's astonishment, she found herself close to her house. She hurried inside at once. Her stepmother and stepsister were delighted to see her – because, of course, she was covered with gold! The girl explained everything that had happened.

"Right, you go and get yourself covered in gold too!" the greedy widow ordered her ugly, lazy daughter. The woman took a thorn and pricked her daughter's finger with it. She let a drop of blood fall on to a spinning wheel shuttle, then she threw the shuttle into the well and pushed her daughter in after it.

Down… down… down… the ugly, lazy girl sank into the well. She, too, fainted. And when she awoke, like her stepsister, she was lying in the meadow. Then she walked along the very same path.

When she came to the oven, the bread called, "Oh, take me out or I shall burn!" But the girl sniffed, "I'm not going to make myself all hot and sooty," and carried on walking.

Then she came to the apple tree, which cried out, "Oh shake me, my apples are all ripe!" But she answered, "Not likely! Apples might fall on my head," and carried on walking.

When she came to Mother Holle's house, she agreed to work for her straight away. The first day, she toiled hard, thinking about all the gold that she would get. But by the second day, she started to be her usual lazy

self. On the third day, she hardly worked at all. And on the fourth day, she refused to get out of bed!

Then Mother Holle was fed up and told her to go home. The girl was very pleased, for she thought it was time for her to be covered with gold. But as she stood beneath the doorway, a shower of thick, gooey, black tar poured all over her. "That's your reward," said Mother Holle, and shut the door.

So the girl went home covered all over with tar – and it was so sticky, she couldn't get it off, as long as she lived.

The Spirit in the Bottle

Once there lived a poor woodcutter. He worked hard from morning until night to save money to send his son to school. The boy worked hard too and became very clever – but the money ran out before he could finish his studies. He had to return home to the woodcutter's hut in the forest.

"I am sorry, son," his father said, "I have no more money to give you – I hardly have enough to buy us food."

"Don't worry, Father," his son said brightly, "I can work hard. I don't mind chopping wood with you."

"But son, you're not used to such hard work," his father said sadly. "And besides, I have only one axe."

"Then see if your neighbour will lend you one, until I can make enough money to buy my own," the lad insisted.

So the woodcutter did and, next morning, the father and son went into the forest

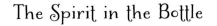

together. The lad got on with chopping wood quite merrily. When the sun was high in the sky, his father said, "Now we will rest and have our lunch."

But his son said, "You rest, Father, I'm going to search for nuts and berries for our dinner," and off he went through the trees.

During his search the lad came to an enormous oak tree. Then it seemed as if he heard a voice. It was very faint, but someone was crying: "Let me out! Let me out!" The lad looked around, but he couldn't see anything. There it was again: "Let me out! Let me out!" It seemed like the voice was coming out of the ground! The boy searched around the tree roots – and there, half buried among the

leaves and moss, he found an old glass bottle.

The lad brushed off the soil and held the bottle up to the light. There was a creature springing and spinning inside! "Let me out! Let me out!" it cried again, louder now and more desperate. So the boy hurried to draw the cork out of the bottle.

The creature slid through the neck of the bottle and began to swell… It grew and grew and grew…

268

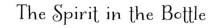

until it became a mighty spirit. It towered over the lad and bellowed: "I was put into that bottle as a punishment. At first, I thought I would reward anyone who released me. But hundreds of years passed and as I waited I grew angrier and angrier – I swore I would kill the next person I met. And that is you – so now you must die!"

The boy was very afraid, but he was clever and he thought fast. "Actually," he said, "I can't see how you can have possibly been shut up in that bottle. You'd never fit inside! It must have been some sort of trick."

"What are you talking about?" roared the spirit. "Of course I was in there!"

"Prove it then," said the lad.

The spirit snorted with annoyance, and at once drew itself up… and shrank and shrank and shrank… until it became so tiny that it could slide back through the neck of the bottle and was once more jumping around inside again.

Quick as thought, the lad grabbed the cork, shoved it into the bottle, and the spirit was trapped once more. He shoved it back among the roots of the tree and went to walk away when the spirit cried out: "Set me free again and I promise you will never want for anything, for

the rest of your life!"

So the boy took out the cork again and the spirit rose out of the bottle and towered over him once more. Luckily, the spirit kept its word. "Here is your reward," it boomed, and it gave the lad a little bag with a sticking plaster in it. "This is a magic plaster," the spirit explained. "Put one end over any wound and it will heal. Put the other end over steel or iron and it will instantly change into silver." In a puff of smoke the spirit vanished and the boy hurried back to his father.

"Where have you

been?" the woodcutter asked. "We should have started work again ages ago."

"Don't worry, Father," soothed the boy, "I will soon make it up to you." He bent over his axe, so his father could not see what he was doing, and rubbed the iron blade with the magic plaster. It turned into gleaming silver! "Look at my axe, Father," the boy said, holding it up. To his surprise, his father looked horrified instead of delighted.

"Oh my goodness, whatever's happened!" the woodcutter gasped. "That's no good for chopping trees any more – silver is softer than iron, it will just bend. I can't give the axe back to my neighbour like that! You'll have to go and sell it – you won't get much for a

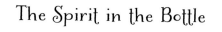

damaged axe though! I'll have to earn however much else we need to buy my neighbour a new one."

"Oh Father!" the son sighed, with a smile. He strode off into town and went straight to a jeweller. The jeweller gave him five thousand pounds for it!

The woodcutter's son went home delighted and asked his father how much his neighbour wanted for the axe. "Ten pounds," the woodcutter said, shaking his head sadly.

"Well, here's ten pounds," said the lad, counting out his money, "and here's many hundreds more!"

"Good heavens!" cried his father. "Where on earth have you got all that money?"

Then the lad told him everything. The old woodcutter was thrilled – not only because he never had to worry about money again, but because his son could go back to school and finish his studies.

So he did – and because he could heal all wounds with his magic plaster, he became the most famous doctor in the whole world.

The Gnome

There was once a king who lived in a palace filled with treasures. But his favourite thing was the beautiful apple tree in his garden. Apples hung from the branches like gleaming rubies. To protect the tree the

king put a spell on it – anyone who picked an apple would sink deep underground.

One morning, the king's three daughters were walking by the apple tree when the youngest one said; "Our father loves us far too much to wish us underground – I bet the spell only works on strangers." She picked a large apple and took a bite – it was delicious! She offered it to her sisters and they tasted it too. But while they were eating, the

ground became soft like sand. To their horror, they sank down and the ground closed over them.

Midday came and the three princesses did not arrive for lunch. The king ordered his servants to search everywhere in the palace and garden, but his beloved daughters were nowhere to be found. The king was beside himself with grief. He announced that whoever found his daughters and brought them back safely would have one of them as his wife.

Then all the men in the land went out into the kingdom, searching high and low.

Among them were three brothers who were huntsmen. They travelled far from their home, looking for the princesses, and reached a great castle. Strangely, the flags were flying and the drawbridge was lowered, but no one seemed to be about. The brothers entered the castle and searched the rooms, but there was not a soul to be seen.

In the great hall, the young men found the table laid with steaming plates of food. They were so hungry that they sat straight down and ate. The three tired brothers agreed that they would rest there that night, and use the castle as a base for the next few days while they continued looking for the princesses.

The following day, the eldest huntsman stayed to watch over the castle while his two younger brothers went out searching. At

noon, steaming plates of food appeared on the table in the great hall once again. Then a strange little man walked in. "May I join you for lunch?" he asked.

"No you can't," said the huntsman, rudely, and he kicked the little man out.

When his brothers returned home the eldest huntsman told them all about the visit from the gnome, and what he had done.

"I'll stay and watch over the castle tomorrow," the middle brother said – and exactly the same thing happened again!

On the third day, the youngest brother stayed. All happened as before, but when the little man said, "May I join you for lunch?" the youngest brother did not refuse. Instead

he replied: "Of course, be my guest."

Then the little man grinned and said: "I
am a gnome and I live underground with my
thousands of brothers. I can tell you where
the princesses are."

He took Hans (for that was the youngest
huntsman's name) and showed him a deep
well. "Take a bell and a sword and go down in
the bucket," the gnome instructed. "You will
find three rooms below. In each one is one of
the princesses with a dragon, whose many
heads she has to comb. To rescue the
princesses, you must cut the heads off the
dragons! But beware your brothers – for they
will be jealous of you and try to get rid of
you." And with that, the gnome disappeared.

Hans returned to the castle and, later on, told his brothers everything – except for the gnome's warning, of course. The next morning, they went to the well together. The eldest brother said it was his right to try to rescue the princesses first. So he sat in the bucket with a bell and his sword and said, "If I ring, pull me up straight away."

The two younger brothers began to lower him down into the darkness. But the eldest huntsman became afraid before he reached the bottom, so he rang his bell and they drew him up again.

Then the second brother sat in the bucket – but he did just the same as the first.

Finally, it was Hans's turn. He sat in the

bucket all the way to the bottom. Then he jumped out, hurried to the first room, and listened outside the door. He could hear the dragon snoring loudly.

He opened the door and there was one of the princesses! She was sitting on the floor, combing the dragon's nine heads. Hans drew out his sword and hacked them off!

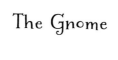

The princess sprang up and kissed him.

Hans went to the second princess, who had a dragon with five heads to comb, and he fought the second dragon and hacked all its heads off. At last he reached the youngest, who had a dragon with four heads, and he killed the last dragon and rescued her, too. All three princesses rejoiced and kissed him.

Then Hans sat a princess in the bucket and rang his bell very loud, and his brothers heaved her up... then the second... and then the third.

When it came to Hans's own turn, he remembered the warning of the gnome. He put a big stone in

283

the bucket instead of himself and shouted that he was ready to be heaved up. Then his brothers began to pull and the bucket began to rise – but when it was halfway up they cut the rope and the bucket fell to the ground and was smashed to bits!

The brothers thought they had killed Hans. They made the three princesses promise not to say anything, then they took them back to the king and each demanded one of them in marriage.

Meanwhile, Hans was wondering how he would ever escape from underground. Suddenly he noticed a strange little silver flute hanging on a hook on the wall. He took it down and cautiously played a few notes on

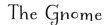

it – and all at once the room was filled with gnomes. "Why have you summoned us?" they all asked.

Hans explained that he wanted to get back above ground again, and asked politely for their help. Immediately the gnomes all took hold of him and, with one great leap, they sprang up out of the earth – and Hans was once again back in the daylight.

He hurried off at once to the king's palace and arrived not a moment too soon, for his bad brothers were just about to marry two of the princesses. All three princesses were overjoyed to see Hans, and they told the amazed king the whole story.

The king ordered the two wicked

huntsmen to be banished from the kingdom at once, never to return. And Hans married the youngest princess and they both lived happily ever after.

The Little Folks' Presents

Once upon a time, a tailor and a goldsmith were travelling together. One evening they heard beautiful music. They followed the sound to see where it was coming from.

Eventually, when the moon
had risen, the tailor and the goldsmith
reached a hill on which they saw a crowd of
tiny men and women. They were holding
hands, swinging round in a happy dance, and
singing sweetly.

In the middle of the tiny people sat a tiny
old man. He beckoned the tailor and
goldsmith, inviting them to join the dance.

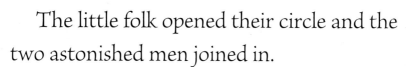

The little folk opened their circle and the two astonished men joined in.

As the dance whirled round, the old man took out a large knife. Before the tailor and the goldsmith knew what was happening, he seized them, one after the other, and in a flash shaved their heads bald! It all happened too quickly for the tailor and the goldsmith to be frightened. The old man clapped them on the back in a friendly manner, as if to say 'well done'. He pointed to a heap of coal nearby and signalled that the men were to fill their pockets.

The tailor and the goldsmith obeyed, although they did not know what use the coal would be to them, and off they went

down the road once more.

The two travellers soon found an inn.
Totally exhausted by their strange
adventures, they sank into their beds and fell
fast asleep.

In the morning, the tailor and the
goldsmith were astonished to find that their
hair had grown back, thicker than ever. They
were even more delighted to discover that
their pockets were filled not with lumps of
coal, but with gold!

The two men were now rich – but the
goldsmith was greedy. That evening, he left
the tailor at the inn and hurried down the
road back to the hill. There were the tiny folk
dancing, just as before. Once again, the old

man signalled for the goldsmith to join in, then shaved him bald and indicated that he should take some coal away with him. The man not only stuffed his pockets, he also filled two bags that he had brought with him. Then, very pleased with himself, he set off back down the road to the inn.

Next morning, the goldsmith hurried to examine his pockets and bags. But to his surprise there wasn't any gold – only coal! He plunged his hands in again and again, but drew nothing out of them but black lumps. How disappointed he was! "Oh well, at least I still have the first lot of gold I collected," he said to himself, and went to examine that. How shocked he was to find that this had

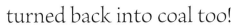

turned back into coal too!

At that moment, the goldsmith happened to catch sight of himself in the mirror. Not only was he still bald, he now had a huge hump upon his back!

Then the goldsmith realized that he had been punished for his greediness and he began to weep and wail. The tailor comforted him, saying: "My friend, don't be upset, I'll share my riches with you." And so

he did. But the goldsmith could never forget
the mistake he had made, for he had to stay
bald, with a hump on his back, for the rest
of his days.

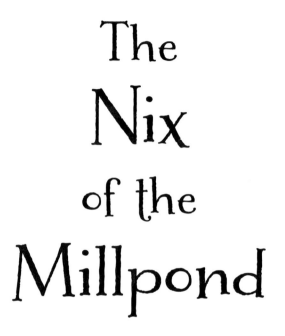

The
Nix
of the
Millpond

Once upon a time there was a very poor miller. Times became so hard that he thought he and his wife might have to sell the mill. He was extremely worried.

Early one sunny morning, he went out for

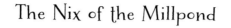

a walk, wondering what he was going to do. Suddenly, he saw a strange long-haired woman rising slowly out of the millpond. It was a spirit – the nix of the millpond.

"I have come to help you," the nix said. "I will make you rich. All I ask is that you promise to give me what has just been born in your house."

'What on earth can that be?' thought the miller. 'A dog or a cat must have given birth in the barn.' He promised the spirit what she asked and the nix sank back down into the water again.

Now the miller felt cheered up and he hurried back to his mill. He rushed through the door and raced up the stairs to his bedroom, to tell his wife the good news. But when he reached her bedside, he stood horror-struck. His wife had just given birth to a little boy!

The miller realized that the cunning nix must have known this and tricked him. He hung his head and told his wife what had happened. She was desperate. "What good is it being rich if we are going to lose our child?" she wailed.

But days went by and the nix did not come to collect the baby. Meanwhile, good luck returned to the miller's house. His business picked up and money began to flow back in. Before long he and his wife were rich. But they were never happy – they were

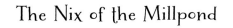

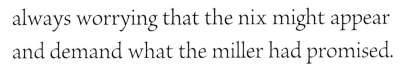

always worrying that the nix might appear and demand what the miller had promised.

As the little boy grew, the miller warned his son never to go near the millpond. "Beware!" he said to him. "If you touch the water a hand will appear and grab you and pull you under."

However, year after year passed, and there was no sign of the nix. The boy grew into a young man and learned how to be a huntsman. He married a girl from the village and the two lived quite happily in their own little home.

One day the huntsman went chasing a deer. When the animal ran out of the woods and into an open field he followed it and

finally brought it down with a single shot. He loaded it on to his horse, then he noticed he was near the millpond and went to the water in order to wash his hands.

Scarcely had he dipped them in when the nix rose up out of the water. Laughing, she wrapped her wet arms around him, then pulled him under so quickly and quietly that there was barely a splash.

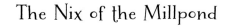

When evening came and the huntsman did not return home, his wife became frightened. She knew what his father had promised the nix long ago and she guessed what had happened. She hurried to the millpond and saw her husband's hunting bag lying on the bank. Crying and wringing her hands, she called her beloved by name, but there was no sign of him. Then she cursed the nix – but she did not appear either. The surface of the millpond remained as smooth as glass. The poor girl paced around it, calling and calling, till she was exhausted. Then she sank down and fell into a heavy sleep.

The girl dreamed that she was climbing upwards between large rocky cliffs. When

she reached the top she found herself in a flowery meadow, where there stood a neat cottage. She walked up to it and opened the door. An old woman with white hair sat there, who beckoned to her kindly...

At that moment, the girl woke up. She decided at once to follow her dream. With difficulty she climbed the mountain – and found everything was just as she had seen it in her sleep. The old woman invited her into the cottage and showed her to a chair. "I can help you," she told her. "Take this golden spinning wheel, then wait till it is full moon and go to the millpond. Sit on the bank and spin until you are out of flax. When you have finished, place the spinning wheel at the

water's edge and see what will happen."

The girl thanked the old woman kindly, took the golden spinning wheel and hurried home. She had to wait several nights until full moon, but finally the shining disk rose in the sky. Then she did just as she had been told. She took the spinning wheel to the bank and span till she had run out of flax. Scarcely had she placed it at the water's edge when a wave rushed up and carried the spinning wheel away with it.

301

Immediately, a huge jet of water fountained up from the middle of the millpond. In it was the huntsman! He quickly jumped to the bank, seized his joyful wife by the hand, and they fled.

They had only managed to run a little distance when there was a terrible roar behind them. They glanced backwards to see the millpond rise up like a massive tidal wave and come crashing down towards them. The swirling waters separated them and carried them far away.

When the waters finally died down, neither of them knew where the other was. For many long years they wandered the land, always searching for each other – and at long

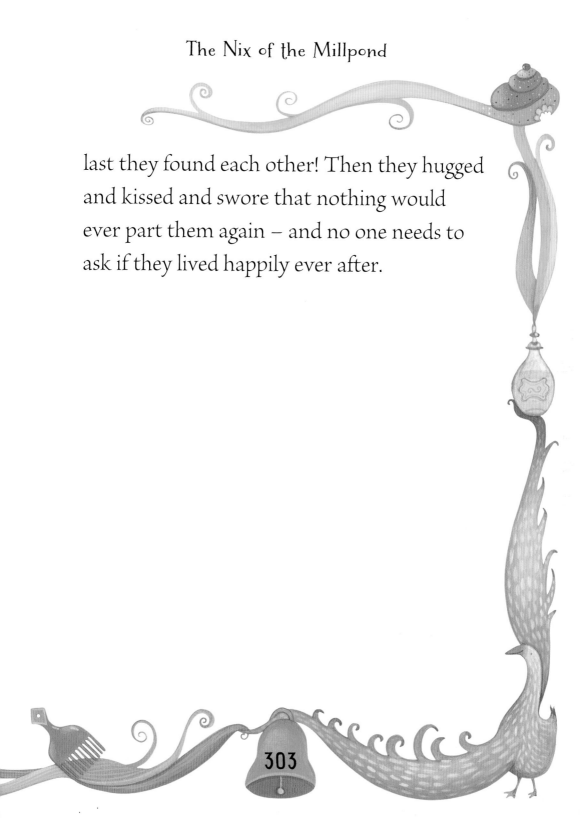

last they found each other! Then they hugged and kissed and swore that nothing would ever part them again – and no one needs to ask if they lived happily ever after.

The Golden Goose

Once upon a time there was a man who had three sons. The youngest son was called Duffer. Everyone thought he was a fool and laughed at him.

One day, the eldest son went into the

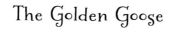

forest to chop wood. His mother packed a cake and some juice for him, so he wouldn't be hungry or thirsty. As he was hacking away at a tree, a little grey-haired old man came up to him. "Can I have a bite of your food and a drop of your drink?" he asked. "I am so hungry and thirsty."

"I've only got enough for myself," the young man answered. "Be off with you!"

The little grey-haired man strode away through the trees. The young man picked up his axe and swung it again at the tree – but he slipped and missed the tree entirely, cutting his leg instead. He had to limp home in horrible pain.

The next day, the second son went into

the forest to chop wood. Again, his mother
packed a cake and some juice for him. The
little grey-haired man came up once more
and, like his brother, the young man refused
to share his lunch. The little grey-haired man
strode away and, with the very next axe
blow, the young man struck himself in the
side. He had to hobble home in agony.

On the third day, Duffer went into the
forest to chop wood. His mother sent him off
with only some dry biscuits and water. He
was hacking away at a tree when the little
grey-haired man came up and asked him for
food and drink. "I don't have anything very
much," said Duffer, "but I will happily share it
with you."

So they sat down, and when Duffer pulled out his biscuits, they had turned into cake, and his water had become juice. So the two ate and drank quite happily together.

When they had both eaten enough the little man said:

"Since you have a good heart, I will give you good luck. Chop down that old tree over there and you will find something precious at the roots." Then the little grey-haired man

strode off, whistling cheerfully to himself.

Duffer did as he had been told and chopped down the old tree. To his great surprise, there was a goose sitting in the roots. But it was no ordinary bird, for its feathers were made of pure gold! He picked her up carefully and went off to an inn where he thought he would stay the night.

Now the innkeeper had three daughters, who couldn't believe their eyes when they saw the golden goose under Duffer's arm. They all wanted a closer look.

That night, the eldest waited till everyone was sleeping, then crept into Duffer's room. She tiptoed over to the golden goose and stroked the wing, thinking she might pull out

a golden feather for herself. But her hand stuck fast! No matter how much she pulled, she couldn't let go!

Not long afterwards, the second girl came creeping in. She too wanted a golden feather, and reached out to stroke the golden goose. But before her sister could say 'Don't touch it!' she too was stuck fast!

Then the third girl came, and the others hissed: "Keep away, for goodness' sake!" But she wasn't listening, she was so dazzled by the golden goose. She reached out to take a feather – and there she was, stuck fast too!

All three sisters had to spend the night with the goose.

In the morning Duffer woke up, picked up

the bird and strolled out with it, not the slightest bit worried about the three girls hanging on to it. They were forced to run after him wherever he went!

In the middle of the fields, they met a vicar who said: "Young ladies, it's not proper behaviour to run after a young man like that – stop it at once!" He grabbed the youngest girl's hand to pull her away. But as soon as he touched her, he was stuck fast too!

Duffer walked on, with the three girls and the vicar trailing behind him. Before long a farmer came by. He was amazed at the sight and said, "Good morning, vicar, where are you all going?" The farmer touched the vicar's sleeve – and he was stuck fast too!

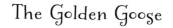

Duffer walked on, with the three girls, the vicar and the farmer trotting along behind him. After a while, they came across two farmworkers labouring in the fields. "Hey, you lads!" called the farmer. "Come and help me!" But as soon as the farmworkers touched him, they were stuck fast too!

Now there were seven people running behind Duffer and the goose: the three girls, the vicar, the farmer and the two farmhands.

Soon they came to a city. In this city lived a king who had a daughter who was so serious that no one could make her laugh. The king had announced that whoever could cheer up his daughter and make her giggle could marry her.

Of course, the minute
the princess saw Duffer
and his golden goose
walking past her
window, with the girls
and the vicar and the
farmer and the
farmhands stuck
fast behind them,
she chuckled and
chortled and burst
out laughing
until tears ran
from her eyes.
The king
couldn't believe

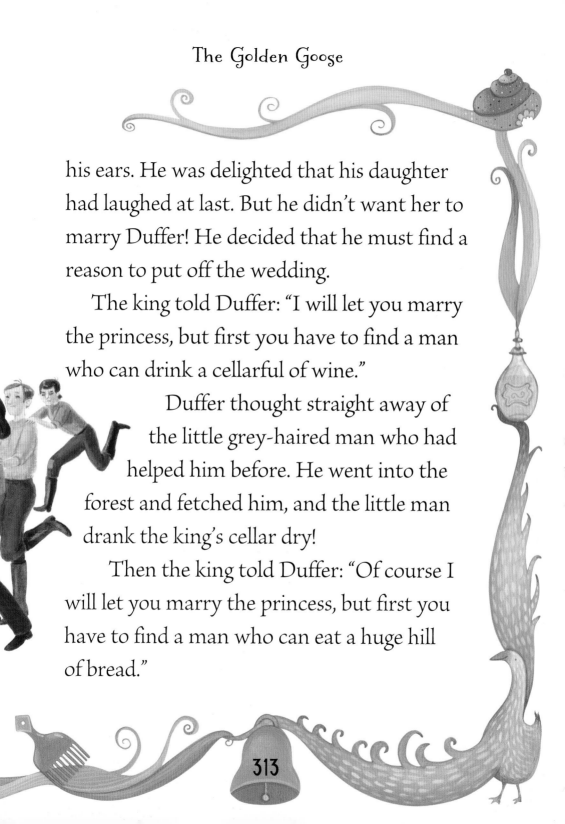

his ears. He was delighted that his daughter had laughed at last. But he didn't want her to marry Duffer! He decided that he must find a reason to put off the wedding.

The king told Duffer: "I will let you marry the princess, but first you have to find a man who can drink a cellarful of wine."

Duffer thought straight away of the little grey-haired man who had helped him before. He went into the forest and fetched him, and the little man drank the king's cellar dry!

Then the king told Duffer: "Of course I will let you marry the princess, but first you have to find a man who can eat a huge hill of bread."

So Duffer asked the little grey-haired man to help him once more, and the tiny fellow ate a massive mountain of bread!

Then the king told Duffer: "I will definitely let you marry the princess, but first you have to find a ship that can sail on land as well as on water."

Duffer asked the little grey-haired man, who snapped his fingers – and a ship that could sail on land and on water appeared.

Then the king saw that Duffer was far from a fool after all – there was no way he was going to get the better of him! The royal wedding went ahead, with much celebrating and rejoicing. The couple lived happily together; Duffer made sure that the princess

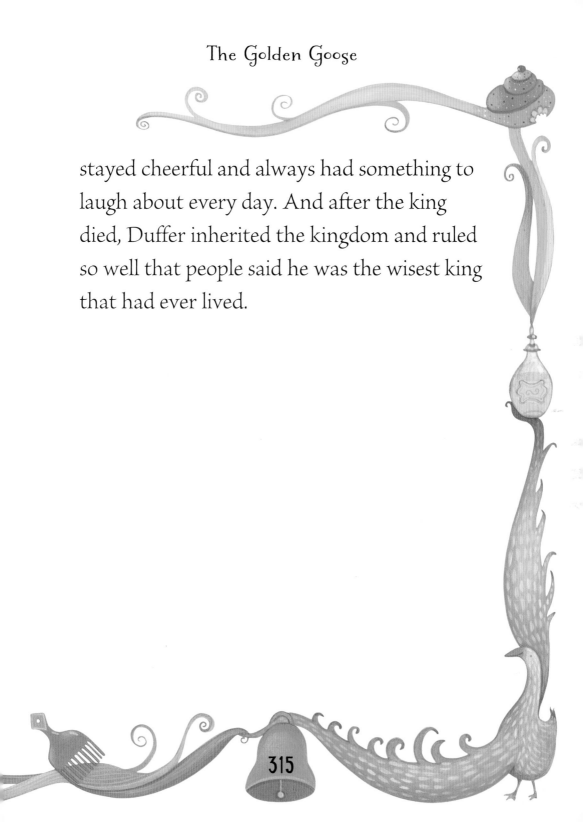

stayed cheerful and always had something to laugh about every day. And after the king died, Duffer inherited the kingdom and ruled so well that people said he was the wisest king that had ever lived.

WICKED WITCHES

Rapunzel

Once, there lived a man and woman who were expecting their first baby. They lived in a little house which overlooked a beautiful garden, full of flowers and herbs and vegetables. However, they never dared go near the garden for it did not belong to them – it belonged to a witch.

One morning, the woman was standing at her bedroom window, looking down into the witch's garden, when she saw a bed of delicious-looking salad. It looked so fresh and green that she wished with all her heart that she could eat some. Every day, her longing for the salad grew – until she found it hard to think of anything else. She became pale and miserable, and her husband began to worry that she might die. So he made up his mind to get her some.

That night, he climbed over the wall of the witch's garden, grabbed a handful of salad and hurried back to his wife. She thought it was the most delicious thing she had ever tasted. But of course it made her desperate for more...

So, the next night, her husband crept back over the wall again. To his horror, there was the witch!

"So," she hissed, pointing her bony finger at the man, "you are the one who has been stealing my salad!"

Trembling, the man explained about his sick, pregnant wife.

"Ah, I see," said the witch, softening. "In that case, take as much salad as you wish – but I have one condition... you must give me your child when it is born."

The man begged and pleaded with the

witch and offered everything else that he and his wife had, but the witch refused. The man knew the witch could do powerful magic. So he promised her what she wanted and fled back home.

Weeks passed and the man took salad for his wife every day. Then came the time when she gave birth to their child – a baby girl. The witch appeared out of thin air, picked up the child and said: "I will take good care of her." Then she disappeared...

The witch called the baby Rapunzel. She wanted Rapunzel all to herself, so she brought her up in a high tower in the middle of a huge forest, far from everything and everyone. The tower had no door or stairs, just a little

window at the top, so the
witch had to magic herself
in and out.

Shut away from the world,
Rapunzel grew into a good,
beautiful girl. By the time
she was twelve, her golden
hair had grown so long and
thick that she could braid
it and let it down out of the
window like a rope, for the
witch to climb up and
down. But there was no
way for Rapunzel herself to
leave the tower.

One morning, when

322

Rapunzel was eighteen, a king's son was riding through the forest when he heard someone singing so sweetly that he followed the sound. It led him to the tower, for the voice was Rapunzel's. The prince rode around, trying to find a way in – but of course, there was no door. He sank down by a tree, very disappointed that he would not be able to see the singer.

While the prince sat, listening, the witch arrived. She didn't notice the prince, and strode to the bottom of the tower and cried out: "Rapunzel! Rapunzel! Let down your hair!" The golden braid came tumbling out of the window and the witch climbed up and went inside.

'Aha!' thought the prince. 'Now I see how it's done.' And he led his horse quietly away through the forest.

The prince waited till evening, then hurried back to the tower. "Rapunzel! Rapunzel! Let down your hair!" he cried, trying to sound like the witch. To his delight, the golden braid came tumbling out of the window and he climbed up and sprang inside.

Poor Rapunzel was terrified! After all, she had never seen anyone but the witch before. However, the prince spoke to her very gently and smiled so kindly that she lost her fear.

The couple talked and laughed and, before the sun rose, they had fallen in love. The prince hurried away before the witch arrived

– for she always came back in the morning – but he promised to return that very night.

And so he did… and the next night… and every night after that. Every time, the prince took with him a skein of silk – for he and Rapunzel had made a plan to run away together. She used the silk to begin weaving a long ladder. When it was ready, Rapunzel would be able to climb down from the tower too. Then the prince would whisk her away on his horse, far out of the witch's reach…

Days went by and Rapunzel's secret ladder grew longer and longer. But one day, while talking to the witch, she completely forgot herself. "You are so slow to climb – the prince is much quicker!" she exclaimed.

The witch guessed at once what was happening – and she was furious! She grabbed a pair of scissors and cut off Rapunzel's braid. Then she magicked the girl far away into an empty desert.

The witch tied Rapunzel's braid to a hook above the tower window. By and by, she heard the prince's voice calling: "Rapunzel! Rapunzel! Let down your hair," and she let the golden braid tumble to the ground.

The prince climbed up the braid – and there was the witch!

"Aha!" she cried. "Now I've got you – and you will never see Rapunzel again!" As the witch began to cast an evil spell on the prince, he leapt out of the tower window. A thick bed of thorn bushes cushioned his fall, so he was not killed – but he was seriously hurt. The sharp thorns pierced his eyes and left him blind.

To the prince, the pain of losing Rapunzel was even worse than the pain of losing his eyes. The poor young man stumbled off through the forest, broken-hearted.

And so the prince wandered over the countryside, living off nuts and berries, for more than a year – until at last he came to the desert where Rapunzel had been banished and abandoned.

The girl could not believe her eyes when she saw him. He was blind and dirty and ragged – but he was her beloved prince!

Rapunzel threw her arms around him, crying tears of joy – and as her tears fell onto the prince's eyes, they cleared. He could see once more! Finally he led Rapunzel back to his kingdom – where they lived happily ever after.

The Goose-girl at the Well

Once, there was a very old woman who lived with her flock of geese in a little hut on a mountain. Everyone said she was a witch.

One sunny morning, a handsome young

count was travelling through the forest. He came across the old woman as she was about to haul two huge baskets of apples and pears onto her back to carry them home. "Good lady," he said, "you'll never manage that – let me carry them for you."

"Thank you, sir," she said. The young man heaved the baskets onto his shoulders and began to follow her to her house.

With every step, the young man's load seemed to get heavier. He hadn't gone far before sweat trickled down his forehead. "Oof!" he puffed. "I'll have to rest for a while." But he couldn't put the baskets down – they were stuck to his back!

"No rest yet!" the witch cried, and she

nimbly leapt on top of the baskets, so the young man had to carry her, too.

Very slowly, the young man staggered up the mountain. He reached the old woman's house when he was just about to drop. The old woman sprang lightly off his back and lifted down the baskets, as her geese ran to meet her. Behind the geese walked the ugliest girl the count had ever seen – she was grey-faced with dull, droopy eyes and lank hair. "Go inside, daughter, and put the kettle on," the old woman instructed, and the ugly girl did as she was told.

The count sank down on a bench by the door, exhausted. Then the old woman said: "Thank you. I have something for you as a reward." She hobbled into the cottage and came back out with a small box. It gleamed and glimmered, for it was cut out of a single emerald. "Take great care of it," she said, "for it will bring you good fortune."

Suddenly the count felt refreshed. He thanked the old woman and set off on his way once more.

Unfortunately for the young man, he got lost in the forest. It took him three days to find his way off the mountain! Tired and hungry, he made his way to the nearest town and presented himself at the castle there, to ask for help. The count was shown into the great hall, where the king and queen were on their thrones. He fell on one knee and offered them the finest thing he had – the emerald box – in return for food and shelter while he recovered from his long journey. The queen was delighted with the gift. But on opening the box, she fainted!

When the queen came to, she began to weep, and explained: "I used to have a daughter who was so beautiful that her eyes gleamed like stars, her hair shone like sunbeams and, when she wept, she cried pearls instead of tears. One day, when she was fifteen, my husband asked her how much she loved him. He expected her to say 'more than the sun' or 'more than diamonds', but instead she said: 'Food tastes horrible without salt, so I love you more than salt.'

"Well, the king didn't think much of that answer at all. He was so angry that he had her banished from the kingdom! The next day he deeply regretted what he had done – but no one could find her. We haven't seen her since. But just now, I opened your emerald box and inside is a pearl just like the ones my daughter used to cry! Please tell me – where did you get it?"

So the count told the queen all about the

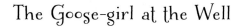

old woman. He said that he hadn't seen or heard anything of the princess. But the queen was determined to go and ask.

Next day, the count set off on his horse, tracing his way back up the mountain, while the queen and king followed behind in a carriage. He led them through the forest higher and higher until the mountain road became very narrow and steep, then he continued on horseback while the king and queen had to leave the carriage and continue on foot.

And so the count came to the old woman's hut first. He stopped to catch his breath under a tree before approaching. There were the geese flapping around outside

– and there was the old woman's ugly
daughter, standing at the well. The girl began
to wash herself in the water, and to the
count's amazement, she peeled off the skin
which covered her face and
head and laid it on the
ground, as if it was a mask.
And then how different she
looked! Her eyes gleamed
like the stars and her golden
hair flowed around her
like sunbeams.

The count thought

she was more beautiful than anyone he had ever seen! He hardly dared to breathe, but stood quite still, and the girl didn't notice him. She carefully picked up her mask and disappeared into the cottage.

The stunned count waited for the queen and king, then told them everything. The couple rushed into the cottage at once. There was the witch, quietly spinning – and there, sitting sewing, was the beautiful princess! For a moment, the girl thought she was dreaming. Then she sprang up and hugged her parents, who were weeping with joy.

"Your daughter has a pure heart – yet you threw her out," the old woman scolded. "She has lived here with me in disguise, so no one has bothered her, and she has been very well looked after. I have kept all the tears that she has cried over you – so now she has a fortune in pearls worth more than your entire kingdom. As my own gift, I give her my cottage…" And with that, the old woman disappeared. The walls of the cottage rattled and a huge cloud of dust flew up. When it cleared, everyone saw they were standing in a splendid palace, with servants waiting to do their bidding…

There is more to the story, but my grandmother, who told it to me, had forgotten the rest. I shall always believe that the beautiful princess married the count and that they lived happily in the palace.

Whether the geese were magicked into the princess's maids, I don't know – but I bet they were. And this is certain – the old woman was no wicked witch, as everyone thought, but a wise woman who meant well. In fact, it was probably her who gave the princess the gift of weeping pearls, when she was born. If only that sort of thing happened outside of fairy tales!

The Lambkin and the Little Fish

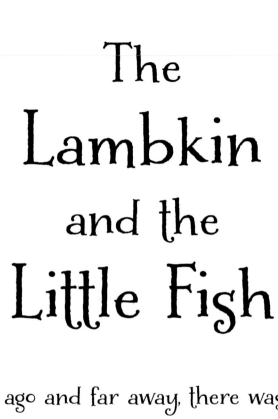

Long ago and far away, there was a rich nobleman who lived in a big castle. His wife had died, leaving him with their two children: a little boy and a little girl. They were good children, who loved each other dearly. But after a few years the nobleman grew lonely and married again. His new wife wasn't sweet and kind and caring like the children's mother. She was miserable and cruel and spiteful – and she was a witch!

One day, the children were running about in the courtyard, playing merrily in the sunshine. The witch stood watching them with hard eyes. Their laughter made her angry – and the more fun they had, the more angry she grew.

Suddenly, she muttered words of magic… *Pfff!* The little boy turned into a fish! The witch picked him up and tossed him into the castle

341

moat. Then… *Pfff!* The little
girl turned into a lamb and
the witch chased her away
into the meadow. The
evil woman turned
on her heel and
strode back
indoors, very
pleased with
her work.

The little fish
swam to and fro in
the pond and was very sad. The lambkin
walked up and down the meadow, and was
miserable. And before the day was out the
witch cast a spell over her husband so he did

not even notice that his two little children were missing.

The next day, friends of the witch arrived at the castle. The woman smiled a horrible smile to herself and summoned the castle cook. "Go and fetch the lamb from the meadow and roast it for dinner for my visitors," she ordered.

The cook did as he was told and went to the meadow and caught the lamb. He was outside the kitchen door, sharpening his knife, about to kill it, when he noticed a little fish swimming backwards and forwards in front of him in the moat. To his amazement, the little lamb cried out: "Oh my brother, I will always love you!"

And the little fish called back: "Oh my sister, my heart is breaking!"

The cook nearly fainted with the shock, but when he recovered, he realized at once that the creatures must be the missing children, under a terrible enchantment. Then he stroked the lamb and whispered, "Don't worry, I won't kill you." He scooped the fish out of the moat in a bucket of water and he hid both the bucket and the lamb in the stable. Then he hurried off to buy meat from the butcher's. The cook served this to the witch and her visitors – and the cruel woman never guessed the difference!

The kind cook waited till it was dark. Then he fetched the lamb and the bucket from the stable and took them into the forest, to a wise woman who lived there in a little cottage. Luckily, the wise woman knew how to undo the spell – and the little girl and little boy were soon back to their usual selves.

Of course, they could never return to the castle again. So the wise woman kept them with her in the forest. She taught them good magic, not black magic – and very happy the children were too.

The
Six
Swans

Once, a king went hunting in the forest. He rode so fast that he left the hunting party far behind. As evening was falling, he realized that he was lost.

An old witch came hobbling through the

trees. "I can show you your way home," she croaked, "but on one condition – you must marry my daughter."

The king looked around him desperately and saw nothing but trees and darkness. With a heavy heart, he agreed.

The witch led him back to her hut, where her daughter was waiting. She was beautiful, but there was something about her that the king didn't like. He lifted the girl up on his horse and the witch showed him the way to the palace, and they were married at once.

Now the king had been married before, but his wife had died. He had seven children – six boys and a girl – who he loved dearly. He did not trust his new wife and thought she might hurt them. So he did not tell her about them. He took the children to a castle which was built on an enchanted road – no one could find it without a special ball of wool that unravelled to show the way. There, the king thought they would be safe.

The king visited his children every day, and the queen grew angry that he left her at home alone so often. She went to the butler and tempted him with gold, and he told her about the children in the hidden castle and where to find the magic ball of wool.

The jealous queen hurriedly made white shirts with an evil charm sewed into each one. Then she waited until her husband went out hunting one day, and fetched the magic ball of wool and set off to the hidden castle.

The children saw someone was coming and, thinking it was their father, they ran out to meet him. But as soon as the queen drew close she threw one of the shirts over each of them. Suddenly they were changed into swans! Off they flew, up into the sky and away.

The queen went home delighted, thinking she had got rid of her stepchildren. But the girl had not run out with her brothers

– and the queen knew nothing about her. Next morning, the brave girl went out into the world to seek her brothers. She walked through fields and over hills until she was exhausted. At last she stumbled across an empty hut in a forest, sank down on a bed there and fell fast asleep.

Just before sunset, the girl was woken by a loud rustling and six swans came flying in at the window. As they landed, all their feathers flew off and their swans' skins fell away. It was her brothers! They were overjoyed to see her. "We are allowed to become human again for just a quarter of an hour every evening," they explained.

"Isn't there any way that I can break the

spell?" the girl asked them, sobbing.

"Yes, but it is too hard," her eldest brother sighed. "For six years you must go without speaking or laughing. And in that time, you must sew six shirts made of white flowers. If a single word escapes your lips, all your hard work will be for nothing."

The quarter of an hour was over all too soon. The brothers changed back into swans and flew out of the window.

Then the brave girl made up her mind to set her brothers free. The next morning, she went gathering flowers and began to sew. She could not speak to anyone – but there was no one for her to speak to. And she could not laugh – but she missed her brothers too much to laugh anyway. All she did every day was gather flowers and sew.

When the girl had been hard at work for several months, a king came riding by. He thought she was very beautiful and asked her who she was and what she was doing. Of course, the sad girl could say nothing. The king's heart swelled with pity and love. He put her upon his horse, gathered up her sewing, and galloped back to his castle.

It wasn't long before the king had fallen deeply in love with the silent, sad girl and married her. But the king's mother was far from pleased. "She may be beautiful," she scoffed, "but what use is a queen who can't say a word!" The woman did all she could to make the new queen feel unwelcome and look foolish.

Months and years passed and still the queen said nothing. Every day, she gathered flowers and worked until her fingers bled, sewing the shirts. Eventually the time came when she gave birth to a baby. One night, while she slept, the king's mother crept into her bedroom. She smeared the queen's nightdress with blood and stole the baby away. Then she told her son that the queen had killed their child!

The king did not believe his mother's story but his chief judge insisted that they must stick to the law – the queen would have to be burnt to death!

The next day – the very same morning that the queen's six years of silence and sewing were finally at an end – a huge bonfire was prepared. The queen had finished all six shirts – except for a sleeve on the last one. She clutched them to her as she was brought out to be burned.

Just as the chief judge was about to light the bonfire, six swans came swooping down through the air. The queen's heart leapt with joy and she threw the shirts upon them, one by one. As the shirts landed on their backs their swan-skins fell off and they were finally back to their human form – all except her youngest brother, who still had a swan's wing in place of one of his arms.

The girl and her brothers kissed each other, crying, and she spoke at last. "Dear husband," she said to the astonished king, "now finally I can speak. I never killed our

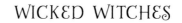

baby! Search your mother's rooms and I am sure you will find him there!"

The king immediately sent servants to hunt for the child and, sure enough, they found him there safe and sound. In his fury, the king banished his mother from the kingdom forever. But he, his queen, their son and her six brothers lived together for the rest of their days in peace and joy.

Snow-white and the Seven Dwarfs

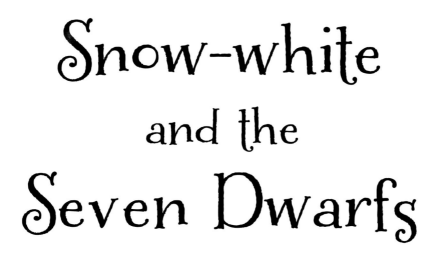

One winter's day, a queen sat by a window, sewing. She accidently pricked her finger with the needle, and saw how beautiful the red looked against the dark ebony window frame and the white snow.

A few weeks later the queen
had a baby girl. She had skin
as white as snow, lips as
red as blood and hair as
dark as ebony. The queen
called her Snow-white.
Sadly the queen
died soon after, and
the king married
again. His new wife was
beautiful but cruel. She couldn't
bear for anyone to be more
beautiful than her. She knew
witchcraft and she had a magic
mirror that she would ask:
"Mirror, mirror, on the wall,

358

who is the fairest of them all?"

And the magic mirror would answer: "You, O queen, are the fairest of them all."

And the queen would admire her reflection and smile.

But one day, when Snow-white was seventeen, the magic mirror replied: "You, O queen, are very fair – but Snow-white is the fairest of them all."

The queen was shocked! Full of envy and hatred, she called a huntsman and said, "Take Snow-white into the forest and kill her. Bring me her heart, as proof."

The huntsman was terrified of the evil queen, and dared not disobey. He seized Snow-white in secret and carried her off to the forest. But he could not bring himself to kill the beautiful, weeping girl! Instead, he told her: "Run away and never come back, for the queen wants to kill you!"

The huntsman slew a young boar and took its heart back to the queen, saying he had carried out her wishes. And Snow-white disappeared through the trees, as fast as her legs could carry her.

She ran and ran until evening began to fall. Then she stumbled across a little cottage and she was so exhausted that she went in to rest. Everything in the cottage was small, but very neat. There was a table laid with seven little plates, seven little knives and forks and spoons, and seven little mugs. Against the wall stood seven little beds. Snow-white ate a tiny bit from each plate and drank a tiny sip from each mug. Then she sank down on a tiny bed and fell fast asleep.

Later that night the owners of the cottage came back – they were seven dwarfs, who had been mining in the mountains for jewels. They were astonished to see Snow-white. "Oh, heavens!" they cried. "Is it an angel?" The little men watched over her all night.

When Snow-white awoke, she was startled to find that she was not alone. But the little men spoke kindly and gently. Snow-white explained what had happened and the dwarfs took pity on her at once. "You are very welcome to stay here with us," they

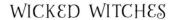

invited, and the grateful girl agreed.

From then on, while the dwarfs went out to work in the mines, Snow-white looked after their cottage and cooked supper. "Beware your stepmother," the dwarfs often reminded her. "She will find out you are not dead and come looking for you. While we are out at work, never let anyone in!"

Months went by and Snow-white was very happy. She and the dwarfs became very fond of each other. But then one day the queen stood before her magic mirror again and it told her: "You, O queen, are very fair – but Snow-white is alive, living with the dwarfs in the forest, and she is the fairest of them all."

Then the queen stamped her feet with rage, for she realized the huntsman had tricked her! She muttered an evil spell and made a magic apple. It looked lovely and tasty – but only the green side was safe to eat, the rosy side was poisonous! Then the queen hissed another spell and, all at once, she was disguised as an old pedlar woman.

She set off into the forest and at length came to the dwarfs' cottage. She knocked on the door crying, "Apples for sale! Delicious, juicy, sweet apples!"

Snow-white put her head out of the window and said, "I can't let anyone in, the seven dwarfs have forbidden me to."

"Do not be afraid, I mean you no harm,"

said the old woman, smiling. "Look, I will eat some first. Then you will see that it is quite safe." The woman drew out a gleaming knife and sliced off the green half of the apple. She munched into it. "See?" she said. "Lovely!"

Then Snow-white could no longer resist. She reached out through the window and took the rosy half. No sooner had she taken a bite than she fell down, dead. The disguised queen laughed a dreadful laugh and hurried back to the palace.

When the dwarfs came home and found Snow-white, they were horrified. They checked to see if she was breathing – but alas, she wasn't! They hugged each other and wept, and all the wild creatures of the forest

wept for lovely Snow-white too.

The dwarfs couldn't bear to bury the girl underground. Instead, they made a glass coffin and laid her in it. They set it outside the cottage in a lovely spot where wild flowers grew and took turns watching over it, so Snow-white was never alone.

Days turned into weeks, and weeks turned into months, but very strangely, Snow-white never changed. She always looked as if she had just fallen asleep.

Then, one day, a king's son came riding through the forest and stopped at the dwarfs' cottage to rest. They sadly showed the prince the glass coffin in which the beautiful girl lay as though asleep. As the prince gazed upon

Snow-white, he fell in love
with her. As he leaned closer
to the coffin, he stumbled and

bumped it. To everyone's astonishment
Snow-white coughed. The piece of apple had
been stuck in her throat and now came flying
out! She opened her eyes and sat up.

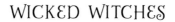

The prince insisted on taking Snow-white back to his palace to recover. It wasn't long before the two were married, and the dwarfs were guests of honour at the wedding.

Meanwhile, Snow-white's stepmother was asking her mirror, "Mirror, mirror, on the wall, who is the fairest of them all?"

The magic mirror replied: "The new queen, Snow-white, is the fairest of them all."

The wicked woman began to burn with fury, so hotly that her magic set her on fire. Before long, she was just a pile of ashes, and she could never harm Snow-white again.

Jorinda
and
Joringel

There was once an old castle in the middle of a large, thick forest. In the castle lived an old woman who was a witch. She had the power to change herself into a cat or an owl. She could also lure wild creatures to her, so she could gobble them up. She had cast a spell around the castle so if anyone came within one hundred paces of it they were struck still like a statue. If a girl was trapped in this way, the witch would change her into a bird and keep her in a cage. She had about seven thousand cages of rare birds altogether!

In a nearby village, a beautiful girl called Jorinda had promised to marry a young man called Joringel. One summer's evening, they went for a walk through the forest. They were so involved in talking together that they did not pay attention to where they were going, and all of a sudden saw that they had strayed too near the witch's castle.

The moment they realized where they
were, Jorinda disappeared and a nightingale
stood in her place, singing sadly. Joringel was
horrifed, but he could not move – he was
frozen as though made of stone.

An owl swooped down from the sky and
flapped into the undergrowth. A moment
later, a crooked old woman walked out, with
cruel eyes and a
hooked nose that
reached almost
to her chin.
She muttered
to herself, caught the
nightingale, and stumped
off with it. Joringel could do

371

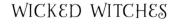

nothing at all to stop her – he could not even cry out!

He stood helpless and, after some time, the old woman came back. All at once, Joringel found he was free and could move once more. He fell on his knees and begged the witch to give him back his beloved Jorinda. But she just laughed and said he would never see her again. Then she vanished!

Then Joringel wept as though his heart was breaking and ran around the forest calling Jorinda's name – but it was no use. In the end, he wandered away sadly.

Joringel thought about Jorinda every day, wondering how he was going to rescue her. Then one night he dreamt that he came across a blood-red flower growing in a meadow. He picked the flower and went to the witch's castle. Nothing could harm him, for the flower broke every evil spell!

When Joringel woke up, he went out searching for the blood-red flower. He looked high and low for eight days, and then on the ninth morning he found the flower growing in a meadow just like the one he had seen in his dream! Joringel picked it with trembling hands, then carried it carefully all the way back and into the witch's wood.

Closer and closer he came to her evil castle – when he was within one hundred paces of it, he found he was not struck still as he had been before, he could keep moving! Then he

was full of joy and strode to the
castle door. It was locked, but he
touched it with the magic flower and it
sprang open. Joringel rushed into the
courtyard and listened for the sound
of birds. There it was! He hurried in
that direction and the birdsong
grew louder and louder.

At last he came to a vast room filled with
cages. The witch was there too, feeding all
the birds! When she caught sight of
Joringel, she jumped up and down
in fury. "How did you get
here?" she screeched.
Claws sprang from her
fingers and poison flew

374

from her mouth. She rushed at him, but when she was just three paces away it was as if she hit an invisible wall – she beat her fists on the air and kicked and screamed, but she couldn't get any closer.

So Joringel drew up his courage and took no notice of her. He strode around the room, inspecting every cage. There were hundreds of nightingales! How would he know which one was his Jorinda?

As he stood there in despair, he noticed the witch quietly creeping towards the door – and she was carrying a cage with a nightingale in it.

Swiftly, he sprang towards the old hag and touched her with the flower. At once, she was frozen like a statue, her powers gone. Next Joringel touched the nightingale with the flower – and Jorinda was standing there, throwing her arms around him, as beautiful as ever! Then they used the flower to turn all the other caged birds back into maidens so they could return to their families.

The pair were married the very next week. The blood-red flower brought them luck in everything they did, and they lived the rest of their days in great happiness.

The Gold Children

There once lived a fisherman and his wife who were very poor. They lived in a tiny cottage. One day the fisherman caught a golden fish in his net.

"Put me back in the water and I will

change your cottage into a castle," the fish promised. So the fisherman put the golden fish back and went home to find a splendid castle standing where his tiny cottage once was. He went inside to find his astonished wife sitting at a table laid with a feast.

However, the couple's luck did not stop there. One day they noticed that outside the castle door, two golden lilies had sprouted. Then a horse in the stables gave birth to two golden foals. Next, the fisherman's wife gave birth to two baby boys who were also made entirely of gold!

The children grew into tall, strong, handsome young men, and they were the best of friends. The time came when they said to the fisherman: "Father, we want to take our golden horses and ride away to explore the world. Watch the two golden lilies outside the door – if they are blooming, you will know that we are safe and well. If they start to fade, you will know that we are in danger or sick. And if the lilies die, you will know we are dead too." With that, they said goodbye and rode off down the path.

The brothers journeyed until they came to

an inn. The people all laughed and jeered when they saw the men made of gold. One of the brothers was so upset by the mocking that he turned round and went straight back home. However, the other decided to keep going. He covered himself and his horse with animal skins, so the gold could no longer be seen. Then he set out once more.

A little further down the road, he came to a village. He saw a girl there whom he thought was the most beautiful girl he had ever seen. He leapt off his horse, walked straight up to her and asked her to marry him. To his delight, even though he was still covered by his animal skins, she fell in love with him too and said yes. The wedding was held that very same day, with much rejoicing.

That night, the young man dreamt he was hunting a splendid stag. It all seemed so real that when he woke up, he told his wife about it and set off into the forest, to see if it would come true.

It wasn't long before the young man glimpsed a fine stag through the trees, just as in his dream. He took aim with his bow and was about to shoot it when the stag ran away. The young man ran after it, over hedges and ditches, for a whole day without feeling tired. But by evening, he had lost the trail. He looked all around him, wondering which was the way out of the forest.

After walking for some time he noticed a

little house among the trees. He approached and knocked at the door, thinking he would ask for food and water. But when it opened, there stood a witch!

"What are you doing walking through the middle of the great forest so late at night?" the ugly old woman croaked.

"I have been hunting a stag," the young man explained.

"What? You've been trying to kill my stag!" the witch screeched. She pointed her finger and muttered some evil words and the young man fell to the ground and was transformed into a large rock. Then the witch laughed to herself and went back into her cottage and slammed the door.

The Gold Children

All through the night the young man's bride waited for him, worrying that something terrible had happened, and in the morning he still had not returned.

Meanwhile, back at the fisherman's castle, the young man's brother noticed one of the golden lilies beginning to droop! "Good heavens!" he cried. "My brother must be in danger!" He sprang onto his golden horse and galloped down the road like the wind – away from his home... past the inn... and into the great forest.

There he found the little cottage and saw the huge stone lying outside – at once, he knew it must be his poor brother.

The witch heard him gasp and came

hobbling out of her house. "I've never seen a golden man before," she called. "Come here, my dear. Let me look at you." Of course, she wished to trap him!

But the young man did not go near her. Instead, he raised his bow and took aim and said: "I will shoot you, if you do not bring my brother to life again."

Then the witch snarled – but she had no choice. She touched the stone with her

384

The Gold Children

forefinger, and the young man immediately changed back to his human shape. He threw off his animal skins and leapt up behind his brother on his golden horse, which sprang away through the forest, like the wind. How the witch howled to see the two golden men escaping her clutches!

So the young man went back to his wife, who was overjoyed to have him back – and

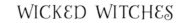

astonished to see him in his true golden form.

And when his brother returned back home, he found the drooping golden lily was standing tall and straight, blooming beautifully once more.

Then they all lived happily for the rest of their days.

The Old Woman in the Wood

There was once a poor servant girl who was sent into the forest to gather herbs. But she wandered off the path and became lost. She began to weep bitterly, crying, "What will become of me?"

She walked about and looked for the road, but could not find it. When evening drew in, she sank down under a tree, exhausted.

Then to her surprise, a white dove came flying up to her – and it had a little golden key in its beak! It put the little key in her hand, and said, "Go to that big tree over there and you will see a tiny lock in the trunk. You can open it with this key."

So the girl went to the tree and opened it. Inside was bread and cheese and milk!

The girl ate and drank and felt much better. "Now is about the time when the hens at home go into the henhouse to roost," she sighed to herself. "I wish I could get into my little bed too."

At that moment the white dove came flying up to her again, this time carrying a second little golden key in its beak. "This key will open that even bigger tree, over there," the dove instructed.

The girl opened the tree and found a beautiful little white bed inside! She couldn't believe her eyes. The girl climbed in under the soft blankets and just had time to

murmer, "Oh thank you, thank you," before
she fell fast asleep.

In the morning, the white dove came
flying up to her for a third time. Again it
brought another little gold key and told the
girl to open a third tree with it. When she did
so, she found beautiful clothes hanging
within. They were embroidered with gold
and jewels, fit for a princess.

Now the girl was much cheered up and
her heart was full of hope.

"Will you do something for me?" asked the
little dove.

"Of course," said the girl at once. "I would
love to pay you back somehow for all the
kindness you have shown me."

"Thank you," said the dove. "I will lead you to a small house. The woman who lives there will answer the door – don't speak a word to her, just go in, passing her on the right side.

Inside the house there is a little door – open it and you will find yourself in a room filled with rings of all shapes and sizes. They will gleam and glitter with gold and silver and jewels – but you mustn't take them. Find the plainest, dullest one and bring it here to me."

The girl hurried after the dove to the little house at once. She knocked at the door and an old woman answered it. Black magic crackled and fizzed all around her, and the girl realized at once that she was a witch, and she felt afraid.

"Good day, my child," said the witch, "how can I help you?"

But the girl remembered what the dove had said and she didn't speak a word in reply. Instead, she did as the dove had asked and pushed past the witch on her right side, and though the old crone tried to grab her the girl managed to slip through her grasp.

She hurried on to the little door and went into the room filled with rings, just as the dove had described. The dazzle of the gold and silver and jewels gleamed like a rainbow in sunshine! The girl began turning them over and over, hunting for the plain, dull one – but she could not find it.

While the girl was searching, she noticed a

movement behind her. She spun round and saw that the witch was creeping out of the cottage, carrying a basket in her hand. The girl raced to the witch and seized the basket out of her crabby old hands. Inside was a little kitten which wore a ribbon round its neck. On the ribbon was a very plain, dull ring.

Quick as a flash, the girl untied the ribbon, took the ring and ran off, out of the house and back into the forest.

She didn't stop running until she was far away from the witch's house. Then she leaned against a tree to get her breath back and waited for the little white dove. She waited and waited – but he didn't come.

Just as the girl was about to despair she

suddenly felt
the branches
of the tree
behind her
move. As they
wrapped around
her waist they
became two arms!
The girl turned
to find that the
tree had become a
handsome young
man! He kissed
her and said:

"That old witch had enchanted me: she put me under a spell where I was a dove for two hours a day and a tree for the rest of the time. By taking her ring you have broken her powers and set me free!"

As the girl smiled with delight, all the trees round about melted and changed into the young man's servants and horses – for they had been enchanted too. Then the young man led them all back to his palace – because he was a prince – where he married the brave, kind servant girl and they lived happily ever after.

Foundling

There was once a huntsman who went into the forest to hunt. While he was riding through the trees, he heard the sound of a toddler screaming. He followed the sound to a high tree and there, at the very top, was a little boy clinging to the branches. The huntsman realized that an eagle must have picked the boy up from somewhere and carried him back to its nest!

He climbed up the tall tree, took the crying child carefully in his arms, and said kindly, "Don't cry. I'll look after you. I will call you Foundling, because I found you. You will live with me and grow up with my little girl, Lina."

And that's exactly what happened. As the years passed, the two children came to love each other dearly. If they ever had to do anything on their own, they were sad until they were together again!

Now the huntsman had an old cook,

called Sara. No one had any idea that she was actually a witch. One evening, Lina saw Sara carrying two buckets back and forth from the spring, again and again. "Why are you fetching so much water?" Lina asked.

"You must promise not to tell anyone!" ordered the old woman. "Early tomorrow morning, while your father is out in the forest, I am going to brew a spell. I need to heat a huge kettle of water to boil up my special ingredient – little boy."

Lina gasped and her eyes widened bigger than saucers, but she didn't say a word. The old woman shuffled off to fetch more water, cackling under her breath.

Next morning, the huntsman got up

before sunrise as usual and went out into the forest. Lina heard him leave – for she was so worried that she hadn't closed her eyes all night. She shook Foundling awake, signalling for him to stay quiet. "I will never leave you," she whispered to her brother.

"And I will never leave you," the little boy whispered back.

"Then trust me. Old Sara is a witch and is planning to kill you! We must run away – *right now.*"

So the two little children got dressed quickly and slipped quietly out of the house. By the time old Sara had got up and had set the huge pot of water to boil, they were well away into the forest.

How furious the witch was when she crept into the children's bedroom and found them gone! She stomped off to the huntsman's servant and yelled: "Those naughty children have run away – fetch them back at once!" And the worried servant set off after the children.

Before long, the little boy and girl heard footsteps chasing after them through the trees. In the blink of an eye, Foundling changed himself into a rose bush and Lina became a rose growing on it. And the servant raced right past them! How puzzled he was, when their footprints suddenly disappeared! The trail was lost. There was nothing for him to do but traipse back home.

"Where are the children?" old Sara screeched when she saw the servant returning from the forest alone.

"I followed their footprints, but they just led to a little rose bush with one rose on it," the servant explained.

Then the old cook roared, "You fool, you should have cut the rose bush in two, and broken the rose off and brought it to me! I suppose I shall have to go and bring them back myself!" And she set off, hobbling and limping into the forest, all the while muttering to herself about how stupid the servant was.

After a while, the children heard the old witch coming. In the blink of an eye,

Foundling turned himself into a pond and
Lina became a little duck floating on it.

When old Sara came huffing and puffing
up, she stopped for a moment at the pond to
take a drink. As she leaned over the water,
the duck seized the witch's hair in its beak

and with one great heave, tugged her right into the water. The old witch drowned.

But the children went home happily together and lived comfortably for the rest of their days.

Hansel
and
Gretel

Long ago, a woodcutter lived in a forest with his two children, a little boy called Hansel and a little girl called Gretel. The children's mother had died, and the woodcutter had married again, but his second wife was an evil woman who did not like Hansel and Gretel.

The family were very poor – so poor that the time came when they didn't have enough to eat. "What is to become of us?" the woodcutter sighed to his wife one night. "We can't feed the children, let alone ourselves."

"I'll tell you what," said his wife, "early tomorrow morning, we will take the children deep into the forest and leave them there. They will never find their way home again and we will be rid of them."

The woodcutter was horrified by this plan, but his wife muttered wicked words into his ear all night until he reluctantly agreed.

The couple had no idea that the children

were awake and had heard everything! Their tummies were too empty for them to sleep. Gretel sobbed but Hansel said: "Don't worry, I know what to do." He put on his coat and quietly slipped out of the house. He collected as many white pebbles as he could fit into a little bag. Then he crept back inside and said to Gretel, "We will be all right, I promise." The children wrapped their arms around each other and sat like that for the rest of the night.

Just before sunrise, the woman got the children up. "We're going into the forest to fetch firewood," she ordered.

She gave Gretel
a chunk of bread to
share with Hansel for lunch, and
off they set. But every now and again, when
the wicked woman wasn't looking, Hansel
dropped a white pebble from his bag, to show
him the way back.

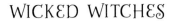

When they had reached the middle of the forest, the woman lit a fire. "Stay here while your father and I go to fetch more wood," she said, and away they walked through the trees.

Of course, they didn't come back. The children waited until night fell, but there was no sign of them. Gretel was afraid and began to cry, but Hansel took her by the hand and followed the white pebbles which gleamed in the moonlight – all the way back home.

Their stepmother was shocked to see them, although she pretended she was delighted and made a fuss of them, saying: "Oh my darlings, I lost you in the forest, I have been heartbroken!" But that night she again told her husband that the children had to go – the very next day, they were to be abandoned even deeper in the forest.

Once again, Hansel and Gretel were awake and heard everything. Hansel got up and went to pick up pebbles as he had done before – but the woman had locked the door!

"Don't cry, Gretel," he told his sister, hugging her. "We'll think of something."

Early next morning, the woman once again gave Gretel a chunk of bread to share for lunch with her brother and led them off into the forest. As they walked, every now and again Gretel crumbled a little of the bread on the path, to show the way back.

Again the woman left the children by a fire and again they waited till nightfall. Then they searched for the trail of bread – but they could find no trace of it! The birds had eaten every last crumb!

"Never mind," Hansel comforted Gretel, "maybe we can find the way on our own."

They walked the whole night and all through the next day – but they could not find their way out of the forest. Then suddenly they glimpsed a little house through the trees. They couldn't believe their eyes! It was built of cake, with a bread roof and windows of clear sugar! The starving children ran to it at once, broke bits off and tucked in. How delicious it tasted!

Suddenly the door opened and an old woman came hobbling out on a stick. She

bent down to peer closely at the two shivering children, for she could not see well at all. Hansel and Gretel were terribly frightened, but the old woman said kindly: "Oh, you dear children, are you lost? Do come in. I will look after you." She gave them milk and pancakes, then showed them to two little beds to rest.

Hansel and Gretel were so tired that they happily went straight to sleep. They didn't know that the old woman was actually a witch who ate children! As soon as the brother and sister had fallen asleep, she seized Hansel and locked him in a cage. He screamed and screamed and Gretel woke up and came running. Then the witch forced

Gretel to fetch water and cook a meal for Hansel, for she wanted to fatten him up, ready for eating.

Every day, the witch forced Gretel to do hard tasks around the house. She had to cook fine food for Hansel, while she lived off nothing but crab shells. Every morning the witch hobbled to the cage and cried: "Hansel, stick out your finger so I can feel if you will soon be fat." And every morning Hansel stuck out a little chicken bone, so she thought he was still thin.

Four weeks passed and the witch grew tired of waiting. "Right, time for a tasty meal of little boy," she announced one day, licking her lips. "First, we'll bake some bread. Girl –

go and climb inside the oven, to see if it is hot enough." The wicked old woman meant to shut Gretel in and cook her first!

But Gretel was clever and said: "Climb inside the oven? I'm not sure what you mean. Can't you do it first, to show me?"

The old witch groused and grumbled and shuffled up and stuck her head in the oven. Then Gretel gave her a mighty push and – *clang!* – she shut and bolted the door. The witch was trapped inside!

The brave little girl raced to the cage and set Hansel free. How they danced for joy! They filled their pockets with the witch's treasure and raced off into the forest.

As they ran, the trees became familiar –

and at last they saw their father's cottage. To their delight, he rushed out to meet them without his horrible wife, for she had fallen ill and died. Their father had been miserable without them – he didn't know how he had ever let his wife leave them in the forest, though he suspected she must have put him under some sort of evil spell. Hansel and Gretel emptied their pockets and showed their father that they would never have to worry about money again. And they all lived happily ever after.

HAPPY EVER AFTER

Cinderella

There was once a rich man whose wife died, leaving him with a daughter. He married again – a woman who had two daughters a little older than his own. However, his new wife was bad-tempered

and spiteful – and her girls were just as nasty.
How cruel they were to the man's daughter!
They took her pretty clothes away and made
her wear an old grey smock and wooden
shoes. She was made to work hard from
daybreak till nightfall in the kitchen, carrying
water, lighting fires, cooking and washing.
They made her sleep by the fireside in the
ashes and, because she was always dirty with
cinders, they called her Cinderella.

Poor Cinderella often felt miserable. Then,
she would slip away to her mother's grave,
where a beautiful hazel tree grew. She would
sit by the grave, under the tree, for a while,
and it always made her feel better.

One day, a trumpeter travelled through

the land announcing news from the king.
There was going to be a festival lasting three
days. All the young ladies in the
country were invited, so that the
prince could choose a bride.

The two stepsisters were delighted
and immediately started to order
Cinderella about. "Clean our
shoes, help us into our dresses,
fasten our necklaces and
bracelets, and do our hair,"
they instructed. Cinderella
obeyed with tears in her
eyes. She would have
loved to go to the
festival too, but

her stepmother had told her she was not allowed. In any case, she had nothing to wear.

The minute the horrid woman and her two ugly daughters had flounced out of the house, Cinderella went to her mother's grave beneath the hazel tree and sobbed.

Just then a little white bird swooped down out of the sky and landed on the tree. It threw down a beautiful embroidered dress and slippers! Cinderella's heart leapt with delight. She put on the dress and hurried off to the festival.

Everyone was at a ball there, dancing. Cinderella was so pretty in the embroidered dress that no one could take their eyes off her. She looked so different from when she was at home that her stepmother and stepsisters didn't recognize her – they thought she must be a foreign princess! As soon as the prince laid eyes on Cinderella he took her by the hand and danced with her. He didn't dance with anyone else all night! And if any other nobleman came to ask her to dance, he said, "No, she is *my* partner."

Cinderella danced till it was late, but she knew she had to be home before her stepmother and stepsisters. If they returned and found her gone, she would be in terrible trouble! When one of the ball guests was talking to the prince, Cinderella managed to slip away. She ran all the way to the hazel tree, and took off her beautiful clothes and shoes and laid them on her mother's grave. The little white bird picked them up and fluttered off with them while she put on her horrible smock and wooden shoes once more. Then she hurried home and took her place among the ashes.

When her stepmother and stepsisters returned, they could talk about nothing but the lovely foreign princess who had danced with the prince all night. "How I wish I could have seen her!" sighed Cinderella, keeping her secret safe in her heart.

The next day, Cinderella once again helped her stepmother and stepsisters into their party clothes. After they had left for the festival she went once again to her mother's grave. The little white bird swooped down with an even more lovely dress and slippers, made of silver cloth!

When Cinderella appeared at the ball in this dress, everyone was astonished by her beauty. The prince had not danced with anyone else, but had waited until she came. He instantly took her by the hand and danced with no one but her. And when other noblemen came to ask her to dance, he said, "No, she is *my* partner."

Once again, Cinderella danced till late in the night and then managed to slip away. The prince looked everywhere for her, but he could not find her! By the time her stepmother and stepsisters returned home, she was once more sitting in her work clothes in the ashes.

Then came the last day of the festival. Cinderella's stepmother and stepsisters went most excitedly, for tonight was the night that the prince would choose his bride.

Cinderella went to her mother's grave one more time and the little white bird swooped down with a golden dress and sparkling slippers even more splendid than before.

When Cinderella appeared at the ball in this dress, no one could speak for astonishment. The prince danced with her only, and if any one invited her to dance, he said, "No, she is *my* partner."

When it became late, Cinderella slipped

away. But the prince had laid a plan. He had ordered the staircase to be smeared with tar. Cinderella was so nimble that she did not stick fast – as the prince had hoped – but one of her shoes did, and she was forced to leave it behind.

The prince smiled as he picked up the shoe, even though Cinderella was running off into the night.

The next morning, the prince set out to find the girl whom the slipper fitted. He went from house to house, but no girl could squeeze her foot into the dainty shoe.

At last the prince came to Cinderella's house. How disappointed he was when he saw the two ugly stepsisters. It was clear that they wouldn't be able to fit their big, flat, clumsy feet into the shoe.

"Don't you have any other daughters?" he asked the rich man, in despair.

"Well… yes – one other," said Cinderella's father, uncertainly. "But she stays in the kitchen – she wasn't at the festival."

The prince didn't care – he demanded to see Cinderella at once.

Nervously, Cinderella went and bowed down before the prince, who gave her the shoe. She seated herself on a stool, drew her foot out of the heavy wooden shoe, and put it into the slipper – which fitted like a glove. And when she rose up and the prince looked at her face he recognized the beautiful maiden who had danced with him! "This is my bride!" he cried. He took Cinderella up on his horse and rode away with her – and they lived happily ever after.

The Bremen Town Musicians

Once upon a time a man had a donkey which he used to carry his corn sacks to the mill. But after the donkey had worked hard for many years, his strength began to fail and he walked more and more slowly with his heavy loads. The donkey realized that the man would soon get rid of him, so he decided to run away. He set out on the road for a town called Bremen. 'I might be able to earn my living there as a musician,' he thought to himself.

The donkey had not gone far when he found an old dog lying in the road, looking sad. "I have grown old and can no longer herd sheep," the dog explained, "so my master kicked me out."

"Come with me," said the donkey kindly. "I am going to the town of Bremen to be a musician – you can be in my band. I'll play guitar and you play the drums."

"Oh thank you," said the dog, cheering up.

And off they went down the road together.

Before too long they met a cat lounging on the path, looking very fed up. "I have grown old and can no longer catch mice," the cat explained, "so my mistress threw me out."

"Come with us," said the donkey kindly. "We are going to Bremen to form a band. You can play the tin-whistle."

"Gladly," replied the cat, breaking into a big smile, and off they went down the road once more.

Presently, they came to a farmyard. The cockerel was sitting on the gate, crowing for all he was worth. "The cook doesn't like my voice," the cockerel explained to them sadly. "She's going to cook me for soup tonight, so I'm crowing while I still can."

"Come with us," said the donkey kindly. "We are musicians going to Bremen. You can sing with our band."

"Cockadoodledoooooooooo!" cried the cockerel, quite delighted, and all four went on their way together.

They were too far from Bremen to reach the town that evening, so they thought they would spend the night in a forest. The donkey and the dog lay down under a large tree. The cat and the cockerel settled themselves in the branches. But the cockerel flew right to the top. Before he went to sleep, he looked around him and thought he saw a little light in the distance. "There must be a house over there!" he called to his friends, and they decided to head for it.

So they made their way towards the light, and soon came to a little house. The donkey went to the window and looked in, because he was the biggest.

"Oh my goodness," he gasped. "There's a table covered with all sorts of good things to eat and drink – and sitting all round it are a gang of robbers!"

Then the animals put their heads together to see how they might be able to drive away the robbers, so they could have the meal for themselves. At last they thought of a plan. The donkey put his front hooves upon the window-ledge, the dog jumped up on the donkey's back, the cat climbed upon the dog, and the cockerel perched on the cat. Then they all performed their music together: the donkey brayed, the dog barked, the cat mewed, and the cockerel crowed – and they burst through the window into the room, so that the glass clattered! Startled by this horrible din, the robbers sprang up, thinking that a ghost had come in, and they fled in a great fright out into the forest.

The four companions were very pleased with themselves. They sat down at the table and ate their fill. Then they each found a resting place and lay down for a good sleep: the donkey settled upon some straw in the yard, the dog curled up behind the back door, the cat stretched out beside the kitchen fire, and the cockerel perched himself upon a beam of the roof.

But the robbers were waiting a little

distance off, watching the house. When they saw that the candles were out and everything appeared quiet, the robber captain said: "We shouldn't have been so frightened!" and ordered one of the gang to go and search the house for the ghost.

They all pushed the youngest robber forward and off he went into the darkness. Quietly, nervously, he tiptoed up to the house. He gently pushed open the door and went into the kitchen to light a candle. But the cat heard the creak of the door and woke up. In the darkness, the robber thought the cat's glowing eyes were coals on the fire. He went over to light a match from the coals and at once the cat flew in his face, spitting and scratching! The robber was dreadfully frightened, and ran to the back door, but the dog sprang up and bit him on the leg. The robber leapt out of doors, but as he ran across the yard by the straw-heap, the donkey gave him a smart kick with its hind foot. The cockerel, too, had been awakened by the noise and cried down from the beam, "Cockadoodledooooo!"

Then the robber ran back as fast as he could to his captain, and said, "There is a horrible witch sitting in the house, who spat on me and scratched my face with her long claws. By the back door stood a man with a knife who stabbed me in the leg. In the yard lies a monster who beat me with a wooden

club. And above, on the roof, sat a ghost who screeched and wailed!

After this the robbers never dared go back to the house again. But it suited the four musicians of Bremen so well that they stayed living there happily for the rest of their days.

King Thrushbeard

There was once a king who had a
beautiful daughter. But she was so proud
that she thought no one was good enough to
be her husband. One day, the king
announced a feast and invited all the young

men from near and far. They lined up in the great hall in rows: the kings first, then the dukes, then the princes, then the earls, then the barons.

The princess went up and down the rows to look at them – but she rejected them all. "He's too tall," she announced. Or, "He's too short… He's too fat… He's too thin… He's too serious… He's too smiley… He's got a big nose… He's got knock-knees…" And so it went on. The princess made the most fun of a king whose chin was a little crooked. "Your chin is like a thrush's beak!" she laughed. "You should be called King Thrushbeard!"

How the princess laughed! But the king was very angry that she was so rude to

everybody. He swore that she should marry the very next beggar that came to the palace.

A few days later a fiddler came and sang outside the palace to earn a few coins. When the king heard him he said, "Bring him in – he shall marry my daughter." The princess pleaded, but the king would not be moved. The two were married, and the princess had to leave the palace with the fiddler!

As her new husband led her away down the road, she wept and wailed, and stamped her feet with anger. They walked and walked until they had left the princess's kingdom and entered the lands of another king. When they came to a huge forest, the fiddler said: "This forest belongs to King Thrushbeard."

And the princess sighed and sobbed, "Oh, if only I had chosen him!"

Afterwards they came to a meadow, and the fiddler said: "This lovely meadow belongs to King Thrushbeard."

And the princess sighed and sobbed, "Oh, if only I had chosen him!"

Then they came to a large town, and the fiddler said: "This bustling town belongs to King Thrushbeard."

And the princess sighed and sobbed: "Oh, if only I had chosen him!"

At last they came to a little hut, and the fiddler said: "This is my house – and your new home."

The princess had to stoop low to go in at the low door. "Where are the servants?" she asked the fiddler.

"What servants?" answered the fiddler. "You must do everything yourself. You can start by making a fire and cooking the supper, for it is quite late." But the princess didn't know how to light fires or cook, so the fiddler had to help her. When they had finished their meagre meal they went to bed, and in the morning, the princess had to get up early to start work again.

For a few days they muddled through like

this, but then they ran out of money to buy food. "Now you must weave baskets to sell," the fiddler told the princess. He went out and cut some willow twigs. The princess did her best to weave the scratchy baskets with her delicate hands – but they weren't very neat at all.

"Now you must sit in the market place and sell them," said the fiddler.

The princess hung her head. 'Whatever will people from the palace think if they see me?' she thought to herself. But she had to do it – or die of hunger.

Unfortunately, the princess didn't manage to sell many of her badly-made baskets. Some people took pity on her because she was beautiful and looked so sad. But still, it was not enough.

"Go and work in King Thrushbeard's palace as a kitchen maid," the fiddler told her. "That way, we will get free food."

Then the princess's shame was complete. She went to work in the royal kitchen, doing the dirtiest, nastiest jobs. Every day, she took home a little bag of leftovers, and that is what she and her husband lived upon.

One day the palace servants were told that the king was getting married. When the wedding day arrived, the princess was kept busy all morning, mopping and scrubbing and fetching and carrying things for the cooks. As the party began she couldn't resist slipping

away to stand near the door of the great hall,
so she could peer in at the wonderful feast.

Candles were lit, plates of delicious food
covered the tables, and beautifully-dressed
guests arrived. The princess wished with all
her heart that she had not been so proud and

horrible to everyone.

All at once the king entered, dressed in velvet and silk, with a gold crown upon his head. When he saw the beautiful girl by the door he took her by the hand, and asked to dance with her. But she refused and shrank away in fear, remembering how she had poked fun at him when they last met!

However, the king smiled at her kindly and said: "Do not be afraid, it is me – the fiddler. I disguised myself in order to teach you a lesson."

Then the princess recognized him. She wept bitterly and said, "I am so sorry – I should never have been so proud and rude!"

The king took her hands in his and said,

"Don't cry – it is all forgotten… and now it is time for us to get married properly."

Then maids-in-waiting helped the princess dress into a beautiful wedding dress. And her father and all his royal court arrived to celebrate the joyful day and wish the couple happiness too.

The Valiant Little Tailor

One summer's morning a little tailor was sitting at his workbench by his window, cheerfully sewing. His tummy began rumbling so he took some bread out of his cupboard and spread a slice thickly with jam. "I'll just finish sewing that jacket before I take a bite," he said to himself. So he left the bread on a plate nearby while he sewed a few more stitches.

The sweet smell of the jam brought some flies buzzing in. "Shoo!" cried the tailor, waving his hand at them. "Go away!" But the flies wouldn't give up and kept zooming around the jam. The tailor grew annoyed and took off his shoe. *SLAM!* He brought it down on the table hard and when he lifted it there were seven dead flies underneath – seven!

"Look at that! I have killed seven creatures with one blow!" the tailor said to himself, admiring his own skill. He set the jacket to one side and quickly ran himself up a belt with the words embroidered on it: *SEVEN AT ONE BLOW*. 'When I wear this, everyone will read what I have done,' he thought with glee, and he locked up his little house and set off to spread the word of his brave deed around the world.

The tailor wandered down a road, always following his own pointed nose. After some time, he arrived at the courtyard of a royal palace. He felt weary, so he lay down on the grass and fell asleep. Some people walked by while he was dozing peacefully. One of them noticed the tailor's belt and read it aloud: "'*SEVEN AT ONE BLOW*'. Ah," he said to his companions, "he must be a mighty warrior." And they all hurried off to tell the king.

The king was delighted and ordered the tailor to be brought before him at once, for he had an important task to give him. "In a forest over the hill there are two giants who are terrorizing my people," the king told the tailor. "Every day the giants go out robbing and murdering people, and burning down their houses. If you can get rid of these two giants for me, I will give you my daughter's hand in marriage and half of my kingdom!"

'That would be a fine thing for a man like me!' thought the little tailor. "Great," he said boldly, "I will do that for you, no problem."

So the tailor set out and soon came to the forest of which the king had spoken. There were the two giants, sleeping under a tree, snoring so that the branches waved up and down. The little tailor quickly and quietly gathered two pocketfuls of stones. Then he nimbly climbed the tree. He perched on a branch just above the sleeping giants and then threw down a stone onto the chest of one. Immediately the giant woke up and gave his friend a shove. "Hey! Why are you hitting me?" he yelled.

"You must be dreaming – I haven't touched you!" the other giant replied.

The pair settled back down to sleep. But as soon as the snoring had begun once more, the tailor threw a stone down onto the chest of the second giant.

"Why are *you* throwing things at *me*?" the

second giant roared, sitting up and pushing his friend awake.

"You must have gone mad," shouted the first giant, "I'm not throwing things at you!"

They argued for a while but they were both so weary that they closed their eyes again. Then the tailor picked the biggest stone out of his pocket and threw it with all his might on the first giant's chest.

"Now you're for it!" the first giant bellowed. He sprang up and punched his friend on the nose. The other hit him straight back – and so it went on, until at last they both fell down dead.

Then the little tailor leapt down from the tree and hurried back to tell the king the good

news. "It is done," he announced. "Now where is my reward?"

So the king, whether he liked it or not, had to keep his promise. And that is how a cheeky little tailor married a princess, won half a kingdom and became a king – all through swatting flies!

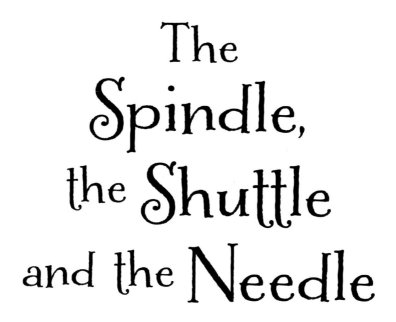

The Spindle, the Shuttle and the Needle

There was once a little girl whose father and mother died. She went to live with her grandmother, who earned a living by spinning, weaving and sewing. The old woman was kind, and brought up the girl to

457

be good-natured and hard-working. However, when the girl was just grown up, the old woman fell very ill. She realized she was dying and said to the girl, "I want you to have my house, so you always have a place to live, and my spindle, shuttle and needle, so you can always earn a living." Then the old lady died.

So the girl went on living in the little house, all alone, and she was able to live on the money she made by spinning, weaving and sewing.

About this time, the son of the king went travelling around the country looking for a bride. He told everyone, "I shall marry the girl who is the poorest and the richest, at the same time." No one knew what that meant exactly, but they did know it meant he was looking for someone very special.

One day, the prince passed through the girl's village. He stopped his horse and peered in through her window. There the girl sat at her spinning wheel, busily working. She looked up and, when she saw the prince, she blushed and cast her eyes down again, and worked faster than ever.

After the prince had rode on, one of the girl's grandmother's sayings came to her lips: "Spindle, my spindle, hurry away, and here to my house bring my sweetheart, I pray."

What do you think happened? The spindle sprang out of her hand, danced out of

the door, and skipped merrily away into the countryside, trailing a bright, shining blue thread after it. Before long, it had entirely vanished from her sight. As the girl now had no spindle, she took the weaver's shuttle in her hand and began to weave at her loom.

Meanwhile, the spindle danced onwards, and it reached the prince. "Whatever have we here?" he cried. "This spindle wants me to follow it!" He turned his horse

around and rode back, following the shining thread towards the girl's home.

There she sat at her loom, singing: "Shuttle, my shuttle, weave well this day, and guide my sweetheart to me here, I pray." Immediately the shuttle sprang out of her hand and leapt out of the door. There, before her eyes, it began to weave the most beautiful carpet she had ever seen. While the shuttle wove the carpet on its own, the girl sat down to sew.

She held the needle in her hand and sang: "Needle, my needle, sharp-pointed and fine, prepare this house for a sweetheart of mine."

Then the needle leapt out of her fingers and flew everywhere about the room as quick as lightning. It covered tables with damask tablecloths, and chairs with velvet cushions, and hung silk curtains at the windows.

Hardly had the needle put in the last stitch than the girl saw the prince coming, following the shining thread. He got down from his horse and stepped over the amazing carpet into the beautifully decorated house. There stood the girl in her poor clothes, but she was so lovely that she shone like a rose surrounded by leaves.

"You are truly the poorest and the richest girl," the prince said to her, taking her hand. "Come – you will be my bride." Then he kissed her, put her upon his horse, and took her to his castle, where the wedding was held with great rejoicing. The girl's spindle, shuttle and needle were stored in the castle's treasure chamber for safe-keeping – and you can see them there still.

The Wolf and the Seven Little Kids

Once upon a time there lived a mother goat who had seven little kids. One day, she wanted to go into the forest to fetch some food. So she called the seven little kids to her and said: "Be on your guard against the wolf – if you let him in, he will gobble you up! If he comes here, he may disguise himself to try and trick you. But you will know it is him because he has a rough voice and black feet."

"Don't worry about us, Mother," bleated the little kids, "we will be fine."

So the mother goat took up her basket and set off into the forest.

After a while, someone came knocking at the door and called out, "Open the door, dear children. It is your mother – I have brought you something tasty to eat."

But the voice was rough...

"No, we will not open the door!" the little kids shouted in reply. "Our mother has a soft, kind, gentle voice. You must be the wolf!"

Then the wolf went away and ate a whole jar of honey, to make his voice soft. He came back, knocked at the door and cried: "Open the door, dear children. It is your mother – I have brought you something tasty to eat."

But the wolf put his black paws up to the window…

"No, we won't open the door!" the little kids shouted. "Our mother has white feet. You must be the wolf!"

Then the wolf loped off to a baker and stole a sack of flour. He scattered it over his feet till they were quite white, then he went for a third time to the house of the little kids.

Once more he knocked and cried: "Open the door, dear children. It is your mother – I have brought you something tasty to eat."

This time, his voice was soft and the paws he put up at the window were white.

Then the little kids believed what he said and opened the door.

The wolf leapt in!

The little kids scampered here and there, trying to hide. One sprang under the table, the second into bed, the third hid in the stove, the fourth ran into the kitchen, the

fifth into the cupboard, the sixth under
the washing-bowl, and the seventh into the
grandfather clock. But the wolf found them.
One by one, he swallowed them up – all
except for the youngest in the clock.

Then the wolf felt full and uncomfortable.
He staggered off and lay down under a tree,
to sleep off his enormous meal.

Soon afterwards, the mother goat came
home from the forest. What a sight she saw!
The front door stood wide open. The table,
chairs, and benches were tipped over, the
washing-bowl lay broken to pieces, and the
quilts and pillows were pulled off the bed. She
searched and searched for her children,
calling out their names, but they were

nowhere to be found. At last, the mother goat found the youngest kid trembling inside the grandfather clock. She took him out and he told her that the wolf had come and had eaten all the others.

How the mother goat wept over the loss of her poor kids!

Then she ran to find the wolf, and the youngest kid ran with her. They found the wolf lying under the tree, snoring loudly –

and something was moving inside his belly!

The mother goat's eyes opened wide. "Could my poor kids still be alive?" she gasped. She sent the little kid home to fetch scissors and a needle and thread. Then the mother goat gently cut open the wolf's stomach. *Pop! Pop! Pop! Pop! Pop! Pop!* Out sprang all six little kids! The wolf had been so greedy that he had swallowed them whole. The little kids brought big stones to the mother goat, who put them in the wolf's stomach and sewed him back up. She did it so carefully that he didn't feel a thing! Then back home they raced and bolted the door.

At length the wolf woke up. The stones in his stomach made him feel very thirsty and he wanted to go to the well to drink. As he walked, the stones knocked against each other and rattled inside him. He reached the well and stooped to take a drink – but the heavy stones tipped him over and he toppled in. The stones carried him down to the bottom and he drowned.

So that was the end of the wolf, and the seven little kids and their mother lived happily ever after.

471

The Goose-girl

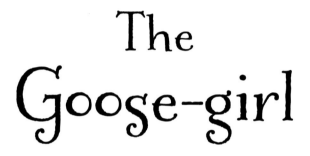

Once upon a time there lived a queen whose husband had been dead for many years. She had a beautiful daughter, whom she loved dearly. When the princess grew up, it was arranged that she should marry a prince who lived in a distant country. It nearly broke the queen's heart to think that the princess would be living so far away, but she knew that the prince was a good man and would make her daughter happy. So the queen gave the princess all the treasure she could possibly take with her as well as a talking horse, called Falada. She and the princess said a tearful goodbye. Then the princess and her maid mounted their horses and galloped away down the road.

After the princess had ridden for a while, she felt very thirsty. She asked her maid to go to a nearby stream and fetch her a drink of water in her golden cup. "Get it yourself!" the girl replied, rudely. So the princess leapt down

from her horse and
went to the stream
to reach the water
and drink.

When the princess
returned to her
horse, she found
her maid sitting in
the saddle. "I will
ride Falada – you
can ride my nag,"
she said, so the princess
had to ride the maid's bony old pony.

Worse was to come. That evening, the
maid forced the princess to swap her royal
clothes for the maid's own shabby outfit and

told her to tell no one – or
the maid would kill her.

So they went on with
their journey – but with
the maid wearing the
princess's clothes and
riding her fine horse, and
the princess following on
behind as the maid.

At last, the travellers
reached the palace. All the
court rejoiced when they arrived
and the prince dashed out to welcome his
new bride. He lifted the maid down from
Falada and escorted her indoors, thinking she
was the princess.

Meanwhile, the old king looked out of the window and saw the real princess standing in the courtyard. He thought she was beautiful and graceful, and hurried to ask the prince's bride who she was. "Oh she's just a maid," the wicked maid replied. "Give her some work to do – she may as well make herself useful."

The king didn't like the idea of the lovely girl doing hard tasks, so he sent her to help a young boy called Conrad look after the geese.

A few days later, the false bride said to the prince, "I beg you to do a favour for me…"

"What is it, my dear?" the prince replied.

"I hate that horse I rode here on," the false bride grumbled. "I want you to have it killed." Of course, she was worried that Falada would

speak and tell everyone what she had done.

The prince was rather alarmed, but he didn't want to upset the young lady just before they were married, so he said yes.

When the real princess found out what was going to happen, she was frantic. She ran to the slaughterman and paid him several pieces of gold to spare Falada. Then she hid Falada in a field just outside the town gate.

Early the next morning, the princess and Conrad drove the flock of geese out through the gateway, to take them to the water meadows. As they passed the field where Falada was hidden the princess said to him: "Alas, Falada, hidden there!"

Then the horse whinnied and replied:

"Alas, young queen, how badly you fare! If this your tender mother knew, her heart would surely break in two."

The princess and Conrad drove their geese into the countryside. When they came to the water meadows, the princess sat down to rest and untied her hair. It shone like pure gold. Conrad thought it was so beautiful that he wanted to pull out a strand for himself. But the princess said: "Blow, blow, thou gentle wind. I say, blow Conrad's little hat away, and make him chase it here and there, until once more I have braided my hair." And there came such a strong gust of wind that it blew Conrad's hat far away, and he was forced to run after it.

When he returned, the princess had
finished combing her hair and had put it up
again, and he could not get any of it. Then
Conrad was angry, and refused to speak to
the princess. So they watched the geese in
silence until evening when they went home.

The next day, everything happened just
the same... And the next... And on the
evening of the third day, Conrad stomped off
to see the king and said, "I won't tend the
geese with that girl any longer!"

"Why not?" asked the old king.

"Because she's so annoying!" said Conrad,
and he told the king all about how the
princess talked to the horse by the town gate
on their way to the meadows, and then made

his hat blow away over the water meadows every morning.

But the old king commanded Conrad to drive his flock out again the next day – and he went and hid by the town gate to see what happened for himself. The king saw with his own eyes the strange things that Conrad had described and, when the goose-girl came home that evening, he called her to him.

Of course, she couldn't tell the king what was going on. "If I do, I will be killed," the princess said sadly, shaking her head.

The old king thought for a while and then said: "If you can't speak to me, why don't you talk to that iron stove over there," and he left the room.

The princess crept over to the iron stove and spoke to it as if it was a close friend, weeping and telling it all the terrible things that the maid had done. Little did she know the old king was standing outside by the stove pipe and could hear everything!

The king hurried back in and ordered his servants to dress the princess in royal clothes – and how beautiful she was! Then he called his son and told him that the girl he thought was his bride was actually only the waiting maid. When the prince saw the goose-girl he fell deeply in love with her at once.

The wicked waiting maid was banished from the kingdom forever, on her bony old pony. A magnificent wedding was held for

the prince and the goose-girl, with great
rejoicing, and they reigned over their land
with peace and happiness.

Iron John

Once there was a king who had a great forest near his palace. No one dared go near it, for whoever did so never came back.

One day a huntsman from a faraway land

arrived. "I will go into the dangerous forest," he told the king, and into the trees he went with his dog.

The dog chased a deer towards a deep pool. When the deer reached the water's edge a strong arm rose out of the water, seized the animal and pulled it under!

The huntsman ran to the pool and looked in. On the bottom lay a wild man, whose body was brown like rusty iron and with hair that hung down to his knees. The huntsman ran back to the palace and fetched guards to help. They jumped into the pool and grabbed the man, then bound him with ropes and led him away to the castle.

The king had the wild man locked into an

iron cage in his courtyard. He forbade anyone to let him out, on pain of death, and gave the queen the key for safekeeping. From then on, everyone called the wild man Iron John, and no one was frightened to go into the forest any more.

Now the king had a son who was twelve years old. He was playing with a golden ball in the courtyard one day when the ball slipped out of his hands and rolled into the cage. "I will only give it back if you unlock the cage and let me out," said the prisoner.

486

Iron John

The little prince really wanted his ball, so he raced to his mother's room and fetched the key. As soon as he had turned it in the lock, the wild man sprang out, gave him the ball, and ran off.

"Stop!" cried the little prince, who realized he was in big trouble. The wild man leapt back, scooped the boy onto his shoulders and ran off again, into the forest.

When they were deep among the trees, Iron John stopped and lifted the boy down. "Don't be afraid," he said. "Do as I say and I will look after you." He took the little prince to a well and said, "Sit here and make sure that nothing falls into it. I will come every evening to check."

So the boy sat by the well and watched, day after day. Years went by and he made sure that nothing fell in. One morning, as he was sitting there, he glimpsed his reflection in the water. How long his hair had grown! He bent to get a closer look – and suddenly his long hair tumbled over his head and dipped into the water. The boy straightened up, fast – but his hair had turned to gold, it was shining like the sun!

When Iron John came that night, he was very disappointed. "You have done wrong and so you must leave me," he said sadly. "But if you ever need help, come back and call for me three times."

The young man hung his head and went

away with a heavy heart. Once he had left the forest behind him he covered his gleaming golden hair with a cap, so no one would notice him. Then he travelled until he reached a great city. There he found work in the palace gardens.

Not long afterwards, war broke out, and the king called for all his warriors to go and fight. "I will go," said the young palace gardener, "just give me a horse!" But the knights and soldiers just laughed at him.

After the troops had ridden off to war, the young man hurried back to the forest and called, "Iron John!" three times.

The wild man came striding through the trees and said, "What do you want?"

"A strong warhorse, please," asked the young man.

To his amazement, Iron John brought him golden armour and a huge horse whose mane flashed with fire and who snorted smoke. Following behind was a great troop of soldiers, their swords gleaming in the sun.

The young man galloped away like lightning to the battlefield – where he found that many of the king's men had already fallen. He and his troop burst like a whirlwind over the enemy and won the fight! But before the king could thank him and find out who he was, he galloped away. He returned the armour and the amazing horse and soldiers to Iron John, and hurried back to his gardener's hut in the palace grounds.

Then the king announced a competition with a special prize. Whoever could catch a golden apple thrown by his daughter would win her hand in marriage. Of course, the king hoped that the mystery warrior would come, so he could find out who he was.

Then the young palace gardener went to see Iron John in the forest once more. "I would like to catch the princess's golden apple please," he said.

"It's as good as done," said Iron John, and he presented the young man with the golden armour and the huge horse one more time.

Next day, all the knights in the kingdom waited on their horses in jostling rows. The

princess threw her golden apple
high into the air. As it span
down, the golden warrior
galloped past them all
on the fiery horse,
caught the precious
apple, and dashed into
the distance. His horse
leapt so fast that his
helmet fell off and
everyone saw his long,
gleaming hair.

How frustrated the king
was, not to know who he was!

A few weeks went by. Then,
one day the princess was looking

492

out of her window and
spotted the young palace
gardener working on his
own. It was a sunny day
and he was obviously very
hot. He looked around him
to see if anyone was watching.
There was no one in sight, so he took
off his cap to cool down.

The princess saw his long,
golden hair tumble to the
ground! She summoned him to
her at once. "You are the
mysterious knight who caught
my apple and who won my
father's battle!" she said. "You

493

can't be just a gardener – who are you really?"

Then the young man explained that he was a prince – upon which the princess kissed him. "I knew it!" she cried, and led him to her father.

A magnificent wedding was soon held for the couple and, to the prince's delight, his long-lost father and mother came as guests. They were just as delighted to see him as he was to see them.

Halfway through the feast, to everyone's astonishment, the music suddenly stopped, the doors opened and a mighty king stalked in, followed by thousands of soldiers.

"I am Iron John," he announced. "I was enchanted to look like a wild man, but now

the spell has been broken. All my riches –
including my golden well – I give to you."

And so everyone was happy for the rest of
their days.

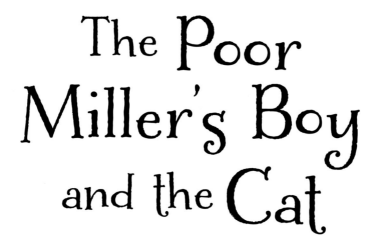

The Poor Miller's Boy and the Cat

Once upon a time there lived a miller who had neither a wife nor a child. Three young men worked for him as apprentices, learning the miller's trade. One day, after they had been with the miller for several years, he said to them: "I am old and cannot work forever. I want each of you three to go out and find a horse. I will give the mill to whoever brings back the best one."

The very next day, all three lads set out down the road on their quest. They walked till it was nightfall without finding any horses. Then they found a cave to sleep in for the night. But the two older apprentices had hatched a nasty plan. They got up while the third, younger, apprentice was sleeping and went on their way, leaving him in the cave.

Eric (for that was the youngest apprentice's name) woke up very upset to find himself all alone. He wandered out of the cave and set off sadly down the road once more. As he walked, he met a small grey cat which said, quite kindly, "Eric, I know what you are looking for."

Eric was too astonished to speak, so the cat continued.

"You want to find a beautiful horse," the cat said. "Come with me and work as my servant for seven years, then I will give you one more beautiful than you have ever seen in your whole life."

'Well, this certainly is an amazing cat', thought Eric to himself. 'Maybe she is speaking the truth…'

So he went along with her to her enchanted castle, filled with cat servants. They leapt nimbly upstairs and downstairs,

and all seemed very happy.

In the evening, Eric and the grey cat sat
down to dinner. Three of the cat servants
played music while they ate: one blew the
bassoon, the other bowed the fiddle,
and the third puffed out his cheeks
at the trumpet.

"Now take him to bed," the grey cat ordered. One cat carried a candle and led Eric to his bedroom. Another cat pulled his shoes off, a second cat took his stockings off, and another cat turned down the bedclothes and blew out the candle.

The next morning, the cats returned and helped Eric out of bed. One put his stockings on, another slipped his feet into his shoes, one washed his face and dried it with her tail. 'Oh, I could get used to this', Eric thought, happily.

But then it was his turn to start work. The grey cat said she wanted Eric to chop wood every day. She gave him a silver axe – and that's what he did. He stayed living with the cats and worked hard, and he was very content. Once, the grey cat asked him to harvest the wheat in her fields. And once, she asked him to build her a small house. And the seven years passed by as swiftly as if they were seven months.

Then the grey cat asked Eric if he would like to see her horses.

"Oh, yes please," said Eric.

The grey cat opened the door of her stables and there stood twelve horses, so bright and shining, that his heart leapt at the sight of them.

"Now off you go back to the mill," said the grey cat, "and in three days' time I will bring you a horse."

Eric trusted the cat and he trudged off

down the road back to the mill.

The other two apprentices had returned long ago, each dragging an old nag behind them. They sneered at Eric and mocked him when they saw him coming. After all, Eric was without a horse – and he was still dressed in the same dirty smock that he had been wearing when they last saw him seven years ago! The two apprentices even said he was too ragged to come into the mill to eat. Instead, they gave him a tiny morsel of supper to have in the barn, where he had to spend the night on the hay.

However, Eric didn't mind.

The next morning, three days had passed since he had left the grey cat. As the sun rose,

a golden coach came driving up to the mill, pulled by six gleaming horses. Behind, a groom rode a seventh.

The coach came to a stop outside the barn, and a beautiful princess got out of it. To Eric's amazement the princess spoke to him. She said: "I was the little grey cat whom you served faithfully for seven years! Now, I will reward you richly for all your hard work."

She clapped her hands for her butler to come forward. He unpacked royal clothes and dressed Eric in them. When Eric was ready, he looked more handsome than any prince! Then the princess strode off to find the miller. She asked to see the horses that the other two apprentices had brought home with them. They were a very sorry sight – one was blind and the other was lame!

Then the princess ordered her groom to show the seventh horse – which she had brought for Eric.

The miller admired the wonderful horse. "The mill belongs to Eric," he said, reaching out for the reins.

But the princess shook her head. "Keep your little mill," she said, "and the horse." Then she showed Eric into her golden carriage and drove away with him. They went straight to the little house which he had built and Eric saw that it had turned magically into a magnificent castle, filled with treasures. He was richer than he could ever have dreamt! There, he and the princess were married, and they lived happily ever after. So let no one ever say that the best stories have sad endings.

The Star Money

Once upon a time, there was a little
girl whose father and mother had died.
She became so poor that she could no longer
afford to live in their tiny house. She had to
go out into the world with only the clothes

she stood up in and one little piece of bread in her hand.

Off the girl went down the road, until she met a beggar-man who said: "Oh please give me something to eat, I am so hungry!" The little girl looked at the piece of bread in her hand and her empty tummy rumbled. Then she looked at the poor beggar-man and saw his pleading eyes.

"Have this with my blessing," she said, and she handed the man her whole piece of bread.

She went a little farther and came to a poor child sitting by the roadside. He was very thin and shivering from the biting wind. "My head is freezing," the little boy moaned, "please give me something to cover it with."

So the little girl took off her hood and gave it to him.

Down the road she went, until she came to another child, even poorer and colder than the first. He stared up at her with dark, sunken eyes in his ghostly pale face.

The little girl took off her jacket and wrapped it around the boy's shoulders, with a gentle smile.

A short way further on, the little girl saw a bundle of rags in a doorway. She drew closer and, to her horror, saw that it wasn't a bundle of rags, but a girl, stick-thin and only wearing tatters. The little girl didn't hesitate; she took off her frock and dressed the beggar-girl in it.

Now the little girl was shivering herself, but she didn't mind. She travelled on into a deep, dark forest. There, among the trees, was another poor, abandoned child. His feet were bare and bleeding, scratched to bits by sharp rocks and thorns. The little girl winced to see them, they looked so painful. She bent down and took off her own little shoes, and offered them to the boy. He took them at once, with heartfelt thanks.

Then the little girl went on her way once

more. Now she had nothing at all – not one single thing left that she could give – and she wondered whatever would become of her.

She looked up at the dark heavens and gazed at the millions of stars gleaming up above. They shone and glittered and twinkled… and began to fall from the sky. The little girl thought she must be dreaming – but there were shining coins falling all around her.

The Star Money

She clapped her hands and laughed with delight, and hurried to gather as many as she could carry.

Then she was rich all the days of her life – and lived happily ever after.

About the Artists

Laurence Cleyet-Merle
Working predominantly in acrylic paint for children's books, Laurence tries to capture the southern light of her hometown of Marseille, France, by using bright colours in her pictures.

Louise Ellis
Passionate about children's books, UK artist Louise works traditionally, using acrylics, watercolours, pencils, texture paste and collage to create her detailed and playful illustrations.

Atyeh Zeighami
From her home in the city of Tehran in Iran, Atyeh works digitally to create her dreamy, surreal illustrations. The biggest source of inspiration for her work is her mother, who is an artist and professor.

Claudia Venturini
Living in Ferrara, Italy, Claudia uses soft, rich colours to bring incredible characters and places to life. Alongside her illustration work she organizes artistic workshops for children.

Martina Peluso
At a very young age Martina read *The BFG* by Roald Dahl and decided that she wanted to be an illustrator of children's books. She was born in Naples, Italy but she loves to travel and currently lives in Scotland.

Ayesha Lopez
As a small child, Ayesha loved to draw – unluckily for her parents this meant drawing on their furniture. Now she combines paper and computer to produce her charming, quirky illustrations. She lives in London, UK.

Kristina Swarner
Often described as magical and dreamlike, much of Kristina's inspiration for her work comes from her childhood memories of exploring old houses, woods and gardens. She lives in Chicago, USA.

Mónica Carretero
Living in the beautiful city of Segovia in Spain, Mónica describes her head as a cabin crowded with characters all wanting to know when she is going to tell their stories and draw them.

Bruno Robert
Following a deep interest in drawing and playing with colours as a child, Bruno now creates sweet, funny, brightly coloured storybook worlds from his home in Normandy, France, where he was born.

Lucia Masciullo
Working in acrylic and watercolour paints, Lucia's dynamic compositions and whimsical characters give her work a fresh, contemporary feel. She lives on the Gold Coast in Australia.

Polona Kosec
Above all things, Polona loves to draw – especially illustrating children's books. She lives in Slovenia, and finds nature very inspiring for her work. She says in this sense she is still a little girl, creating magical worlds with colours.